Confounding variables in a psychotherepeautic relationship

Why psychotherepeautic goals go wrong!

Confounding variables in a psychotherepeautic relationship

Confounding variables in a psychotherepeautic relationship

Dedicated to my mentor the late Jock Sutherland

Contents

I have learned far more from my failures than succeses ! -Jung

There is nothing like a failure in psychotherapy as each such 'failure' imparts wisdom!- Jock Sutherland

The Author

Professor Ashoka Jahnavi Prasad is a trained psychiatrist who also has a doctorate in philosophy and is an Academician with the prestigious American Academy of Arts and Sceinces.

THE IMPERFECT THERAPIST

What Is Failure?
Definitions of Imperfection

Therapists come under attack by insurance companies, review boards, medical colleagues, the media, public consumer groups, litigation attorneys. Can we demonstrate that we really make a difference in people 's lives? Is anybody actually helped by our interventions? With malpractice premiums doubling every few years and increased legal actions against clinicians, we cannot even trust members of our own profession for fear we will be called upon to testify against one another. This atmosphere of inquisition makes it all the more difficult to discuss our prob - lem clients, our confusing or bungled cases, our misgivings and mistakes. So we often choose not to confront the doubt that lurks within.

Psychotherapy, like most service professions, is performance-oriented. Clients understandably get upset if they do not feel better soon, or at least eventually. In a competitive marketplace where preferred provider organizations (PPOs) and health maintenance organizations (HMOs) are springing up, and where professional specialties and theoretical orientations are competing for attention , clients are becoming more critical consumers and more demanding of perfection. Those therapists who are unsuccessful in their helping efforts, or who even admit to the occasional lapse in sainthood , will often experience a loss of confidence by their colleagues and clientele.

Furthermore, failure is seldom discussed in the literature. After making an error in judgment or a strategic mistake, many of us feel too guilty and vulnerable to air our dirty laundry in public. And certainly journal editors must agree that the therapist's imperfections should be ignored or buried since little research with nonsignificant results is ever published. There is a considerably higher rejection rate for studies that report null results and a general bias against those dealing with negative outcomes (Barbrack, 1985). This attitude is reinforced by our teachers and supervisors who broadcast their brilliant breakthroughs and miraculous cures, but never seem to err or lose a client.

In one of the few works ever written about treatment failures, Foa and Emmelkamp (1983) speculate about why the subject has been largely ignored. If the therapist has made an accurate diagnosis and case analysis, has applied appropriate and generally accepted procedures, success is supposed to be inevitable. Since the diagnostic system and treatment approach have already been endorsed as effective, the belief has been fostered "that if one encounters a treatment failure, then one is a failure as a therapist" (p. 3).

In light of our exposure to literature that radiates positive outcomes and the successes of our mentors, we may come to believe we are alone in our self-doubt and uncertainty. But when we confide our concerns with colleagues, we find that they have the same fears and imperfections that we do. We learn much more from our own and others ' mistakes than we do from success. We remember the mistakes clearly—the clients we failed, the families we inadvertently alienated, the missed cues and misdiagnoses. No doubt every therapist could instantly name a case that did not work out and offer all sorts of reasons why this was so. Probably much time and energy went into thinking about this case and scrutinizing it for errors. Thus significant attention is indeed paid to failure, even though it may not be discussed or written about.

Given the widespread reluctance to discuss mishaps and mistakes, given a professional environment that is suspicious and vigilant, given our self-doubts and the cynicism of an impatient public and disdainful critics, there are few places we can turn to find relief or enlightenment. If very few of us ever talk about our imperfections and failures for fear of the consequences, how are we ever to improve our effectiveness and come to terms with our human fallibility?

After their study of common therapeutic errors, Robertiello and Schoenwolf (1987) conclude that most failures are caused by the clinician's character flaws or narcissism: "We t herapists must come forth and acknowledge the existence and persistence of a great deal of psychopathology in ourselves and must drop our defensiveness. We must recognize counter-transference and counter-resistance as universals—not rare phenom ena that only appear in a few aberrant, deviant therapists" (p. 286). It is the premise of this book that embracing failure is essential to the therapist's well-being. Our focus is on the therapist's experience of failure and the learning that emerges from an exploration of this subjective experience: how the therapist lives with and through failure.

The literature on failure seems to search for "variables" in the client, the therapist, or the therapeutic environment that might prevent negative results. While this is, of course, of utmost importance in our profession, the underlying message remains the same: " If you work hard enough, and learn more, you won 't experience defeat." This notion that failure is negative and can somehow be avoided has been part of our secret mode of operation for years. The following disclosure is a case in point.

Accepting Imperfection

1 (J.K .)* feel scared every time a client walks through the door for the first time. No matter how much deep breathing or head clearing 1 do, the same thoughts pop into my mind: Will t he client like me? What if he has a problem I don 't know any t hing about? Will this be the one who finally discovers I don 't really know what I'm doing?

Once the client sits down and we begin, there is little t i me to continue with my self-doubts, at least until the session ends and I remember all the things I could have done or said. It is then, while composing my progress notes, that I realize how

*When first-person anecdotes are offered, we use our initials (J.K. or D.B.) to identify which one of us is speaking.

littl e I know about what is going on with this client or what to do about it.

Certain admonishments from former supervisors might enter the picture at this time: "You 're not supposed to know what to do, but help **them** know what to do " or "Take your ti me, you 'll know what 's going on eventually ." I have never t aken much comfort from this advice; always with me is the shadow of self-doubt. With every client I feel that I am once again putting myself on the line. I must bring all my skills and learning to bear. I must be willing to risk—to take a leap of faith —for while 1 might indeed experience success, I might just as easily face failure.

Although I think of this success or failure as being **mine,** in truth it is the client who has everything to lose or gain. This person in therapy has chosen to be with me because of a belief t hat 1 can make a difference. I feel the weight of this confidence, its presence and pressure, moving me to dip once again i nto a well of resources. I breathe deeply. We begin.

Most of the time a truly miraculous event does indeed occur—the more time I spend with the client, listening to his heartbeat, the more I get a sense of what is disturbing him, the context of these symptoms within his past and present, and even a pretty good idea of the best way to be helpful. Yet hav‐ ing lived through this experience a thousand times does not seem to help. My reputation , my confidence, my very sense of competence as a person —everything seems to be on the line with every new client I see. No matter how many clients might leave treatment feeling as if I have helped them , I still wonder: Will I be able to do it again?

Imperfection is inherent in our work. In the words of one psychoanalyst struggling to live up to his own expectations and t hose of others: "All of us feel less than perfect—because we are. All of us feel vulnerable, because the human condition is a vulnerable one. All of us want more than we possess—more love, more money, more prestige. Because every human being feels li mited and **is** limited, he seeks someone who will make his life as perfect as possible. Men and women who go to a psychoana ‐ lyst hope he will be in the image of a perfect parent who can

restore to them the lost paradise of infancy " (Strean and Freeman, 1988, p. 8). In spite of these unrealistic expectations, we
have no reasonable choice but to accept our imperfections.
Sharing the therapist's foibles and flaws affords each of us a rich
opportunity for learning and growth that will enable us to practice our profession more realistically and come to terms with
our fallibility.

In the Pulitzer Prize novel **Lonesome Dove,** two cowboys
argue on the merits of an occasional failure. Augustus accuses
his friend Call of being too stubborn to ever admit he is wrong:

> "You 're so sure you 're right it doesn 't mat-
> t er to you whether people talk to you at all. I'm
> glad I've been wrong enough to keep in practice ."
> "Why would you want to keep in practice
> being wrong ? " Call asked. "I'd think it would be
> something you 'd try to avoid ."
> "You can 't avoid it, you 've got to learn to
> handle it," Augustus said. "If you come face to
> face with your own mistakes once or twice in your
> life it 's bound to be extra painful. I face mine
> every day —that way they ain 't usually much worse
> t han a dr)' shave" [McMurtry, 1986, p. 696],

Preserving the Therapist's Ego

It does not take much to set off a therapist's relapse with
failure. Our best-kept secret is the fear that we do not really do
anything —that clients would improve anyway if left to their
own devices. This is why we often feel defensive initially (wheth - er
we show it or not) when we encounter a client's resistance or
criticism. While it is true that the client should get credit for the
success of treatment, it is the therapist who is blamed when
things plod along. This phenomenon is all too readily apparent in
the following episode.

I (D.B.) gently placed the receiver back in its cradle and
leaned back in my chair to give my pulse a chance to slow
down. The initial shock gave way to a profound feeling of loss

and disappointment. "I'm canceling Rudy 's next appointment. We're scheduled to meet with another therapist."

I had been seeing Rudy, age fifteen, for over a year. I had worked closely with him and his parents in an effort to reduce his violent outbursts at home and school. Things had been going quite well (or so 1 believed). His attitude had changed. He had become calmer and the frantic phone calls from his parents slowly diminished. I was therefore stunned by this unexpected bombshell and the nagging question inside me: How had I failed?

The lump in my throat finally abated only after I began an intricate series of self-justifications and rationalizations, the most effective of which involved discrediting the parents ' reasons for stopping the treatment. Surely the fault rested with t heir incapacity to understand their son and inability to tolerate his adolescent rebellion! Since he had been improving, their own family system must have destabilized and they needed to sabotage the therapy so they could regain their own peace. A fellow family therapist I consulted readily agreed this is what probably happened and concluded : I t 's not your fault.

Having succeeded in easing my conscience, I reviewed Rudy 's file and carefully scanned it for clues I should have no - ti ced (all the while readying myself to dispute any indications of an error on my part). I have a well-developed repertoire for dealing with such situations by using the client's resistance, mo - ti vation, defenses, or meddling family as possible excuses. These explanations, as usual, worked fairly well. I exonerated myself, li berated myself from culpability, then distracted myself by t hinking about other clients who I knew valued me and were in- deed making progress under my tutelage. Avoidance. Escape. Relief!

Would honest scrutiny of all the evidence have made a difference? Willing to see myself clearly in a realistic light, what could I have learned had I not so quickly avoided self-confron- t ation? For indeed a failure with Rudy had felt like a personal failure as a therapist; it had the potential of bringing me to an inescapable awareness of my own fallibility as a person and as a professional. It no longer had to do with Rudy. Now it involved t he opportunities I had missed for learning and growing, for

considering other therapeutic options, and, most of all, for con −
fronting my own unrealistic need for perfection.

During my training I was able to gather bravado and gain
applause as I carefully presented cases to teachers and supervisors. I knew what to say, what to omit, what to emphasize so
t hat I could avoid any criticism I did not want to acknowledge.
I was skillful at manipulating my training to protect my ego. I
felt as if I was in control—doling out just the right amount of
self-criticism and self-awareness. But in my office I did not have
t his control. If I did, Rudy would still be in therapy with me
and would not have gone elsewhere for something more, some−
t hing better, something I believed I had failed to provide.

In reflecting upon my work as a therapist, 1 became
aware of the energy I invest in viewing my cases from a perspective that protects my ego—of interpreting a client's behavior not
as a reflection of my skills but, more safely, as a reflection of
t heir impairment and resistance (which sometimes is indeed the
case). I teach my clients to forgive themselves (and others), to
accept themselves as they are, to embrace their weaknesses as
aspects of their uniqueness, to welcome their failures as oppor− t
unities for learning. Yet this valuable wisdom I do not so easily
apply to myself as an imperfect therapist and flawed human
being. 1 have great trouble forgiving myself, embracing m y
weaknesses, welcoming m y failures.

The Drive to Succeed

Most of us were programmed for success by our parents
and mentors who instilled in us a great drive to achieve. The
t r aining of a therapist begins during infancy, not graduate
school. From a very early age many of us were indoctrinated
i nto the family role of rescuer or mediator. We developed a high
degree of compassion; yet we were also taught to respect power
in relationships. We were instilled with a drive for success—if
not monetarily, then certainly in our ability to charm or per−
suade. We prized books, growth , learning, above all else. At
home, in school, in the neighborhood , many of us were encour−
aged to pursue our calling as saviors of the suffering. We came

t o believe that anyone can do almost anything —most of all, our-selves.

Throughout professional training our egos became ever more intimately connected with achievement and success. An excellent grade, a professor's approving nod, a supervisor's com - pliment, a client's innocent gratitude would send us into somer-saults of elation. Those of us who survived the trials and tribula - t i ons of graduate school believed ever more in our brilliance and our uncanny ability nor only to succeed but to help others to do so as well.

The problem is that under the guise of not compromising our morale, we were often sheltered from the experience of confronting failure. Seldom were we exposed to the disasters and mishaps that are part of every practice. We were shown bril-li ant ideas for producing dramatic cures. We were presented with books and films that highlighted exceptional cases of im - provement. We were given recipes for success without the prepa - ration for processing our failures. When confronted with cases like Rudy, quickly we close the door to self-scrutiny, to honest exploration of what we did and could have done differently had we not been so concerned with preserving our hungry egos.

Defining Failure

It is obvious from the preceding discussion there are diffi-culties in discerning what constitutes a failure in therapy. If Bertrand Russell could say that mathematics, the most exact of all disciplines, "may be defined as the subject in which we never know what we are talking about, nor whether what we are say-ing is true" (Zukav, 1979, pp. 98 -9 9), then what can we ever hope to claim regarding psychotherapy , the most scientifically primitive of all professions?

If the client felt all right about the way things were going, and the therapist agreed that things were moving along on schedule, then is it the parent paying the bill who ultimately decides whether the treatment is working? Or if you do every- t hing right, just as anyone else would handle the case, and the client elects to kill himself—is this a failure?

What about those instances in which a client has made clear and consistent progress over a period of many months, but refuses to acknowledge that she is in any way different? We have all seen such improvement in a client who very' slowly and surely lets go of maladaptive behavior and becomes somebody quite different—all the while stubbornly maintaining that the t herapy just is not working. In spite of obvious changes we might see, and even those observed by a client's relatives, the client refuses to acknowledge success. Sometimes the changes are just too gradual to notice in oneself, and because the focus is on continued change, the client does not see what has been accomplished, only what still remains as a block to growth. Other times the client simply refuses to believe the therapy has worked because of a reluctance to accept continued responsibilit y for change. If the client were to admit that she is a pro ─ foundly different person, she would have to relinquish her favorite excuses blaming others for her plight or saying "I can 't help the way I am ." And it could mean the client must end t herapy and terminate a relationship that perhaps has no substit ute in her world.

A second common scenario that confuses definitions of failure and success occurs when a client believes (or claims to believe) that he is completely cured and will no longer require our services even though we can observe only minimal changes. This may happen just at a time when we thought we were gett i ng close to something significant, so close, in fact, that the client's fear of the unknown provoked a hasty retreat. Schlight (1968, p. 440) describes what he considers an incredibly anxiety-provoking task —that is, the evaluation of progress:

> Very often the views of the patient and the ther─
> apist on this question are at odds; frequently other
> persons in the patient's life may complain that the
> patient is getting worse at a time when the therapist
> feels the patient is improving. Of course, we know
> t hat all parties concerned have somewhat different
> axes to grind, so naturally they see the "progress"
> slightly differently. The answer to this problem of

measurement of progress depends ultimately upon
a value choice, and the choice has to be made es-
sentially by the patient and therapist acting togeth -
er, with more or less regard for the significant oth -
ers in the patient's life and for the rest of society.

Each of these examples highlights the difficulties in defining our subject because of the universal problem of measur-
ing therapy outcomes. Since it is difficult even to define the
exact nature of a client's presenting complaint, there is no clear
understanding of what constitutes success or failure in the first
place. We cannot, therefore, specify anything other than vague
objectives or determine if and when they were ever achieved
(Strupp, 1975).

Mays and Franks (1 9 8 5) explain further why the study of
failure is so difficult. First, we cannot prove causality. If a client
gets worse, how do we know it was because of the therapist's
action? People in therapy are often unstable, in crisis, teeter-
ing on the edge because of outside pressures. Second, there are
relatively few reported cases of failure, making it hard to accu-
mulate a large enough sample to study. Third, there is not only
reluctance to report cases of failure because the clinician would
lose face and credibility, but even if there were a large sample,
it would be unethical to manipulate experimentally negative
outcomes. These scientific limitations are further exacerbated
by others of a more philosophical nature. In a complex essay on
t he linguistic implications of unfortunate consequences, Theo -
bald (1979) distinguishes between what constitutes a mistake
versus an error: "To sum up, then, mistakes describe our failure
t o apply a certain accepted method carefully to a given prob -
lem, while errors describe our failure to employ the right meth -
od in the solution of that problem" (p. 561).

And while we thought failure quite simply involved not
doing something we set out to do, such actions can be classified
in no less than eight different categories. According to Margolis
(1960) we can "fail to act" —that is, we can be frozen with fear
and thus not deliberate in our "actlessness." This type of failure, for example, could apply to unexpected crises in which
some action is demanded that we are unable to perform . This

variety is to be distinguished further from "failing to take action" in which some effort or decision needs to be made —such as the failure of a government to act. Another way of failing occurs when we begin an activity but do not complete it because of a change in mind or heart. There are others as well: "failing to try hard," "failing in what one wishes," "failure of what one does" versus "failure of what one has tried to do."

We draw consolation from the realization that however we may address this subject, we can never fail in **trying** to do something. Success or failure can only apply to a judgment regarding an outcome —that is, whether the result is what we intended. According to Kouw (personal communication , 1988), failure is a kind of "honorable ignorance" that is not necessarily a negation of the therapist's good intentions.

Who Defines Failure?

Clinicians can shrug off these questions that have confounded therapy researchers for generations, but we cannot hide from the personal demands of our own moral integrity. When things go wrong —and inevitably things will go wrong some time in the near future to compromise our image as flawless wizards—therapists must find some way to explain why things did not proceed as planned.

In their survey of seventy-five prominent therapists, Strupp and Hadley (1 9 8 5) define failure in therapy as a worsening or exacerbation of suffering and symptoms characterized by any of the following: depressive breakdown , confusion , lowered self-esteem, increased guilt and inhibition, diminished impulse control, erosion of interpersonal relationships, acting out, excessive dependency on the therapist, or disillusionment with the therapy process. In describing their greatest sources of stress, 264 therapists who participated in a study by Deutsch (1984) listed the following indications of failure: premature termination, suicide attempts, a client's expression of dissatisfaction, lack of observable progress, not liking a client, self-doubts about effectiveness, opinion of a consulting colleague, a client who constantly misses appointments, or not meeting our expectations.

Failure in therapy is clearly a subjective assessment. It is

t he meaning and value the therapist attributes to his or her involvement with a client. Hyatt and Gottlieb (1987) define failure as a judgment about an event. It is neither a permanent con -
dition nor a statement about a person 's character; rather, it is a
t r ansition stage that consists of an awareness that one 's performance in a certain area could be improved. It is based on the
t herapist's expectations of a particular client and for his or her
participation in that client's life. It reflects the therapist's belief
t hat the client can and will change and that the therapist has
t he ability, in some way, to facilitate such change. Indeed, perhaps one reason why therapists avoid looking at failure is a need
t o preserve their faith in their client's potential as well as their
own.

How a therapist explains an event is influenced by several
factors according to Jenkins, Hildebrand, and Lask (1982).
They emphasize the relevance of internal (blaming oneself) versus external (blaming others) attributions. Therapists may blame
t hemselves totally for what has occurred and generalize this specific experience of failure to their overall competence as a clinician (such as our disclosures mentioned earlier). Certainly the
t herapists' view of themselves, their level of competence and
confidence, their vulnerability to disappointment, mediate
strongly in their assessment of their work. For many therapists,
however, lack of client change is blamed exclusively on the client. Unfortunately , in either extreme, blaming oneself or blam -
ing others, relevant learning is unlikely.

The therapists '   theory of practice holds implicit expecta -
t i ons for change, its signs, the time frame in which it is to occur,
and who carries the responsibility for it. The psychoanalytic
model, for example, deals with changes that are intangible and
t hus immeasurable, downplays symptomatic relief, provides a
flexible and lengthy time frame, has a well-articulated and de -
tailed treatment plan that allows the therapist to sense that
progress is being made even if it is not observable or felt by the
client, and puts responsibility for success on the client. By con -
trast, strategic family therapy encourages the therapist to assume responsibility as the expert in relieving the symptoms over
a designated period of time.

Most therapists and clients define success as taking place when they both feel better (or believe they feel better). This condition represents one end of a continuum in which subjective reports of progress may be acknowledged by the client or t herapist. The only clear indication of failure is when both parties agree there has been no apparent change in feeling, thinking, or being. The word "apparent" in the foregoing sentence has special significance in the struggle to distinguish between positive and negative outcomes. Some theorists postulate that t he whole concept of failure is more apparent than real. Failure occurs when one has not accomplished what one set out to do. Yet, throughout history, many a so-called catastrophe has resulted in spectacular success.

Columbus, for example, was utterly a failure in not having completed his intended mission of circumnavigating the globe and finding a shortcut to the East Indies. During his maiden voyage he resorted to trickery and deceit to avoid mutiny by his homesick crew. He falsified his ship 's log by cutting in half the distance he believed he covered each day, never realizing that in his attempt to make the trip seem shorter to his sailors, he was compensating for his own tendency to overestimate distance t raveled. By luck, accident, and a series of miscalculations, Columbus ended up in Cuba rather than Japan , which has to be one of the most monumental failures in history.

Even after three more voyages without seeing a single Oriental face, Columbus could only offer feeble, progressively more ridiculous excuses for his inability to find the Orient. With uncanny accuracy he kept navigating to the same region and discovered a lot of interesting places—Puerto Rico, Trinidad, Haiti, Jamaica, Costa Rica, the Antilles. Still he remained a failure, convinced until his death that he had found Asia by sailing around the world in thirty days (Boorstein, 1983).

Hobman (1953 - 5 4) concludes, after studying dramatic failures throughout history, that they are all relative and even necessary for later successes: "When after aeons of evolution from the original speck of life, fish first began to emerge out of t he waters, how many million of such creatures must have perished before some at least managed precariously to survive on

t he slime in the open air?" (p. 184). Continuing this metaphor
of how failure eventually facilitates growth in nature, Thomas
(1979) remarks on how nature 's mutations and lapses are what
caused us to evolve from a primitive though perfect microbial
cell: "The capacity to blunder slightly is the real marvel of DNA.
Without this special attribute , we would still be anaerobic bac⁻ t
eria and there would be no music " (p. 28).

Unrealistic Expectations

What leads us to the calling of psychological healer?
Altruism and idealism certainly play a part, as do more personal
motivations involving control in relationships. Yet the narcissistic search for perfection —attaining a state of complete serenity
and well-being—permeates our lives and our work with clients.
Many of us thus became therapists (deliberately or unconsciously) to relive our imperfect childhoods, to fix families that re-
semble our own, to rectify our historical mistakes by teaching
clients what we have learned, to experience a control over oth ⁻
ers' lives that we never felt as a child, to work through inherited
guilt by giving back to the world whatever we feel we have already taken, to become immortal by having our wisdom and
i nfluence live forever in the spirits of those we have helped
(Kottler, 1986). In any case, therapists are notoriously hard on
themselves when they do not live up to their unrealistically high
standards of success.

We are often seeking reassurance that we have not lost
our power, our magic, whatever it is that allows us to be effec⁻
tive. No matter how many years we have practiced, how long
we have studied, how many accolades we have received, how
many cures we have facilitated, no matter how busy our prac⁻
t i ce is or how many referrals come our way, we are vulnerable
t o the depression and anxiety that accompany a sense of failure.
Our esteem is that much more fragile because it is so hard to tell
how we are really doing. Are we successful as long as clients
keep returning for more sessions? Are we successful when clients like us enough to send their friends? Are we successful only
when we believe ourselves to be?

No matter what criteria we use to measure our performance, we therapists never quite live up to our expectations.
Some of our clients will not improve significantly no matter
what we do —no matter what any therapist could do. And by
t he sheer number of subtle and direct interventions we make in
a single session we are bound to make mistakes eventually. Any
isolated five-minute interval would have us attending to a mul-
t i t ude of stimuli pouring in—the client's posture, tone, expression, surface and deep verbal structures, not to mention the
clock and grumbling stomach. We pick up some of the material
and context, probably miss more than we catch, sift through
t he possibilities available to us (all the while missing more data
flowing in), and then choose from a hundred options ranging
from a simple grunt or nod of the head to a complex metaphor.
Then whatever we decide to do (or not do) presents a problem
in execution since we can never be perfectly articulate and elegant. There is always some way, upon reflection, that we could
have done or said something better.

This nonstop self-critical monologue can take a brutal toll
of the therapist's illusion of perfection. Dr. Fine, a psychoana -
lyst from a novel by Samuel Shem (1 9 8 5) who strives just once
in his life to complete the elusive perfect session, makes it all
t he way through a fifty -minute hour without uttering a single
word —a formidable accomplishment, he believes, since he has
not erred even once. He revels in his achievement, so caught up
in his ecstasy that he wishes his patient a good day as she walks
out the door, thereby ruining what could have been an unblem -
ished event!

Fine 's absurd preoccupation with conducting the perfect
silent session exemplifies the impossible standards that therapists sometimes set for themselves. Hilfiker (1 9 8 4 , pp. 64-65)
l aments how the medical profession, in general, has no place for
mistakes, for doctors must bear the yoke of perfection with no -
where to face their guilt: "Because doctors do not discuss their
mistakes, I do not know how other physicians come to terms
with theirs. But I suspect that many cannot bear to face their
mistakes directly. We either deny the misfortune altogether or
blame the patient, the nurse, the laboratory, other physicians,

t he System , fate —anything to avoid our own guilt." It is not only doctors who expect perfection from themselves. It is also t he patient—desperate, despondent, fearful, who tries to believe in the healer's omnipotence. "But the degree of perfection ex − pected by patients is no doubt also a result of what we doctors have come to believe about ourselves, or, better, have tried to convince ourselves about ourselves" (Hilfiker, 1984, p. 62).

According to Bergantino (1985) the situation is made worse since relationships in psychotherapy , like all human affil-iations, are destined to fail; they can never fulfill the ideals of perfection that are expected. There are no perfect relationships, only a degree of satisfaction and a certain amount of disap-pointment. "I do my best to shatter all the images a patient has of what our relationship should be and force him to attend to what it really is" (p. 42). Naturally, once the client experiences t he therapist as an authentic human being, fraught with flaws, he can begin to accept the self as imperfect as well as the reali− ti es of other relationships.

Perfect Case Examples

Even the best therapists make bad decisions, misjudge or distort what is occurring in a session, or commit the cardinal sins of psychoanalytic lore —that is, to be seductive (promise more than you can deliver) or sadistic (deliver more than you promised). Yet in the pursuit of fame and fortune therapists t end to exaggerate what they can do and minimize what they cannot do.

When presenting a case in a staff meeting, we tend to re-late the details that enhance our image as diagnosticians. Rarely do we admit the "weakness" of being confused. In one such case conference attended by a dozen various social workers, psychologists, psychiatrists, and counselors, as well as another dozen interns, participants take turns demonstrating their bril-l i ant grasp of the neurological, psychodynamic, and familial-social dimensions of each case. Finally, the time comes for the i nterns to discuss the clients they are having trouble with. Utter silence. Not one of these beginning clinicians wishes to admit t hey are confused and do not have a complete grasp of what is happening with every client on their caseload. In fact, they present only those clinical issues they can talk intelligently about. Nobody wants to be seen by their peers and supervisors as "deficient."

When we stumble in a session, nobody else but the client will ever know (and he is usually too self-absorbed to notice). When a referral source calls for a consultation , we often hide our ignorance about a particular subject and pretend a wisdom we do not possess. In the pursuit of professional recognition it is important to appear infallible and unflappable, to pretend a confidence we do not feel and a universal expertise we do not have. Just as Dorothy got very upset when she discovered the Wizard of Oz was only human , clients in therapy sometimes become demoralized and disillusioned when their wizards exhibit human foibles.

In one sense psychotherapists are a genus of the world species of witch doctor. We are a bit more refined, but no less confident, and not much more effective than an Ethiopian spirit doctor, Peruvian curandero , Puerto Rican espiritista, Navaho medicine man, Hindu guru, Tanzanian mganga, or Nigerian healer. We are faith healers. We all cure people of their suffering by capitalizing on our power, prestige, communication , sensitivity, and rituals while playing on the client's expectations and trust. All healers work by naming what they think is wrong (diagnosis), assigning meaning to the suffering (interpretation), and intervening in some therapeutic way   (herbs, medicine, reinforcement). Torrey (1986) further elucidates the personal qualities of the universal "medicinal mensch " in all too familiar terms. While not all witch doctors are unconditionally accepting, they all exhibit the personality traits most admired by their cultures. Therapists, in every society, believe in themselves. They are reserved, respected, feared for their special knowledge, even t hought to be in consort with some higher power. Failure is death for the healer. Once a client does not improve, the therapist is held responsible and thought to be negligent or impure in some way.

Dropouts in therapy occur most often when the client's

unrealistic demands are not immediately satisfied. After twenty years in a dysfunctional relationship a couple will complain to t heir marriage counselor after four sessions: " I'm sorry, but this doesn 't seem to be helping. We've told you our history, shared our feelings, and you 've told us some interesting ideas. But things are just the same. We still fight a lot. And our sex life stinks."

In all parts of the world therapeutic sorcerers refuse to accept responsibility for failure. Not only would their reputa‐ t i ons be sullied, but in some cases the healer might be dismissed, banished, or even killed. Torrey (1986) explains that all ther‐ apists have good excuses to protect themselves. While we might blame the client's rigid defenses or disqualify the case as "un ‐ suitable for treatment ," the witch doctor cleverly ends sessions by invoking some taboo that will inevitably be broken , thus allowing an escape. When we tell a client, "I guess this means you aren 't ready to change yet , " we are, of course, creating our own exit clause. Admitting to failure jeopardizes our prosperity, weakens our power and respect in the eyes of the public, and undermines our confidence in our ability to cure.

In workshops, classrooms, books, videotapes, movies, and television, master clinicians bedazzle their audiences with wit and wisdom . They relate cases of instant cures and hard ‐fought victories in which the client finally saw the light, his resistance worn down , and lived happily ever after —all because his brilliant t herapist did the right thing at the right time. As students, we could not help but be impressed by these wonderful case his‐ tories in which the therapist knew exactly what to do and everything worked out perfectly. Coleman (1 9 8 5) also marveled during her training years how the experts used quite different theories and techniques with the same unqualified success.

Since we desire to have others see us in a favorable light, we relate our victories and embellish our successes. Not that we exactly lie to our students when we tell them about our latest stunning breakthrough . Rather, we just do not want them to be disappointed when we tell them the ways we have stumbled. They might lose confidence in us. Moreover, we might then lose confidence in ourselves.

Yet, as we are all well aware, failure is often rewarded with far better results than a modest success. Consider, for ex - ample, the interpretations that are embraced by clients versus t hose they reject. The easiest way for a resistant client to dis- arm the most eager therapist is to comply and agree with your i nterventions: "Yes, Doctor, that 's a good point " or "Yes, you 're certainly right"—which are just patronizing ways of saying, "Sure, sure. But I can 't change." On the other hand, interpre - tive failures require discussion, debate, often heated responses from clients to correct our misperceptions. Langs (1978) em - phasizes the value of honest acknowledgment and exploration of an error in technique and argues that "these errors, when cor- rectly understood and resolved, can lead to some of the most human and moving experiences possible between patient and t herapist" (p. 154). A therapeutic faux pas can sometimes pro - voke anger or doubt in our skills, but often it stimulates deeper exploration and understanding.

In building a case for the uses of failure in therapy, we are suggesting that we need not be perfect specimens with brilliant case histories to be effective clinicians. It would be better, too, if we therapists could divulge our doubts and disasters. We are personally more interested in what consistently does not work for others than what does. We want to know about other 's ex- perience with failure—not only because we feel less alone in our own self-doubt but because we have found prohibitions to be more universally applicable than simple truths.

2

Fear and Avoidance
of Failure in Therapy

Failure, although a commonplace experience of life, is a neglected area of study in psychology. It is treated more as a literary or historical subject that traces the rise and fall of civilizat i on rather than the decline of individual accomplishment. Alt hough failure is a prevalent theme in literature, music, and art, in our own field its attention is restricted solely within the narrow perspective of psychopathology . "The unpleasantries and pain it causes may account in large measure for its neglect as a subject of investigation" (Rochlin , 1965, p. 226).

Conspiracy to Deny Failure

Psychologists, doctors, social workers, nurses, and coun – selors alike are reluctant to deal with their failures. We are much more apt to complain about others ' mistakes; rarely do we acknowledge our own. "Unable to admit our mistakes, we physicians are cut off from healing. We cannot ask for forgiveness, and we get none. We are thwarted , stunted ; we do not grow " (Hilfiker, 1984, p. 62).

Kilburg (1986) notes that professionals can be their own worst enemies by not readily acknowledging when they are in t r ouble. Whatever else they become, they must be a winner. He says, "Admitting they have self-doubts is tantamount to pro – claiming they have failed" (p. 25). Is it not ironic that this attit ude of invulnerability is so widespread among people who are t r ained to help others with their problems?

Millon, Millon, and Antoni (1 9 8 6) speak of therapists ' re– l uctance to admit failure and the part our clients contribute to

20

this resistance: "Because of the great emphasis on self-reliance and professional autonomy , there exists an unspoken expecta - t i on that healers should need no healing. This tacit standard is reinforced by a parallel and equally unrealistic expectation on t he part of patients. Viewing themselves and being viewed by others as paragons of mental health prevents needy psycholo - gists from admitting weakness and seeking help " (p. 131). There seems to be an unspoken agreement among helping profession- als to cover their own reputation by blaming others. Defensive documentation is the name of the game, creating progress notes t hat are designed to provide evidence of the therapist's compe- t ence rather than useful material to work on in the future:

> "The patient has been informed of his rights and has agreed to waive them ."
> "The patient's parents were notified of her suicidal idea- t i on and agreed to assume responsibility for monitor - ing her behavior."
> "It appears as if his symptoms have been inaccurately diagnosed by previous doctors. Decompensation may occur in some future time as a result of this omission ."

It is hard to imagine the record would ever reflect what really happened, without defensiveness or attempts to explain away t he outcome: "At a time when the client really needed reassur- ance from me, I was daydreaming and completely missed the cues he was sending as pleas for help. I blew it."

In discussing the conspiratory neglect among therapists who refuse to deal with their failures, Graziano and Bythell (1983) quote the authors of a book on mistakes in behavior t herapy: "Our traditional American response to failures is to re- j ect them , to consign them , metaphorically or actually, to the refuse heap where they are expected to decay and disappear i nto our tolerant environment like all our wastes and useless by -products."

Clients are fearful of admitting their therapy might not be helpful since they would be acknowledging defeat of their last hope. Therapists refuse to admit failure to avoid losing face t o themselves and to others. Agency administrators use creative auditing techniques to ensure that failure rates remain appropriately low. We therefore have a situation in which everyone wants to believe that things are working out much better than t hey seem. Since there are few corpses or other physical evidence indicating a bungled case, why not assume the best? Everyone stays happy —clients because they can believe, at least for a little while, that maybe they are not really falling apart and getting worse with every session; therapists because they do not have to confront their mistakes and misjudgments; and administrators because they will gain approval from a high success rate, even if the data are distorted .

The Big Questions

The conspiratory neglect of facing failure is pervasive, not only in the field but in the evolution of a therapist's life. At different ages and professional stages we become vulnerable to different crises in our work. This is a complex structure, however, and while we can name discrete periods in the process, there is considerable overlap between them . However we might describe t he therapist's fear of failure, whatever model we might invent t o explain why it exists and how it is responded to, there are several nagging questions that form a part of every therapist's professional conduct and emotional world.

What I f I Don't Have What It Takes? This fear echoes   through   -
out graduate school and professional training. This is not to say t hat our insecurities did not play a significant role before we began our calling. As indicated in Chapter One, there are a myriad reasons why one enters the profession. Stoltenberg and Delworth (1987) describe most therapist trainees as "neurosis-bound " because of apprehensions related to evaluation by their supervisors. They are audiotaped , they are videotaped, their sessions are critically viewed. While striving for independence and competence, they feel insecure, confused, and terrified of failure. Ever-present evaluation of their professional adequacy colors the graduate school experience with unrelenting anxiety.

Questions about one 's abilities can be heard in the incessant inner whisperings of graduate students: What if I don 't have what it t a kes to be a therapist? Maybe I 'll say something stupid in class and everyone will know I don 't know what I'm talking about! What if I mess up my internship? What if I can 't stand the pressure? Who would hire me? I don 't know what I'm doing! While not everyone is suited for the role of therapist, those that make it have survived the rigorous scrutiny of professors and peers and enter the field already vulnerable to rejection and fearful of making mistakes.

Anderson (1 9 8 7) refers to this early period as a search for heroes that is motivated by an overwhelming need for answers. An interesting phenomenon grows out of this preoccupation . Capable students become too greatly revered while their less effective counterparts are intensely criticized. Fueled by their fears of failure, students latch onto friends and faculty mentors and constantly measure themselves against this sometimes un – realistic standard. We overcome this first stage of fear only after we stop comparing ourselves to our mentors and peers and feeling we fall short. We realize there is a difference between theory and practice. It is not only what we know that counts, but rather how we can be with someone. We learn that the brightest students do not necessarily make the most effective helpers, t hat if we try hard enough, care enough, and are honest with ourselves, we can become proficient in helping clients to feel safe and valued when they are with us. It also helps to discover t hat we know more and can do more than we thought at first.

We are so accustomed to having our therapeutic responses analyzed, rated, and judged that it feels strange to discover that even our most awkward attempts to be helpful seem to go smoothly in the client's eyes. And when we do offer a few reflections or interpretations, they will be greatly appreciated. Almost never will the client interrupt us by suggesting we use deeper-level interventions or that we be more concise. After awhile, we no longer expect to be confronted and corrected. We realize that even if we do not have the ideal qualities and train – ing of the perfect therapist, our clients do not seem to notice. We begin to recognize and value our own resources and strengths.

Shortly after my m other 's death, I (D.B.) returned to my office to face a full day with clients. Having been away for a few weeks and in an attempt to catch up, I had scheduled one client after another, leaving little opportunity for a break. By t he time the second client of the day was sitting across from me, I realized that my ability to concentrate was waning. It was t aking more and more energy just to stay focused. I wish I could say that at that point I altered my schedule to suit my needs, but instead I plowed on, compelled to finish the day as planned.

What is most striking about this experience is how well t he clients did despite my lack of presence. And, in fact, for the ensuing weeks they continued to thrive while I struggled through my own grieving process and its impact on my work. While I was not there as fully as I had thought necessary, I discovered t hat what I was offering my clients was sufficient to facilitate t heir progress. Competence is not synonymous with perfection.

What I f I D on 't Know What to Do? The

second stage in the dread of failure is an outgrowth of these early insecurities. We develop a fear of uncertainty —a fear that when a certain prob − lem or kind of client walks through the door, we will not know what to do. Although this fear emerges quite often during the early stages of our career, even the most seasoned veteran can experience a relapse of symptoms.

Just last month , after 1 (J.K .) thought I had treated nearly every variation of depression and anxiety that exists, not one but tWO new referrals walked in—both labeled by the courts as exhibitionists. Never having worked with such cases before, and remembering enough from my training to know that therapy is seldom successful with impulse disorders, I started to panic. "Oh, no, I don 't even know where to begin. They don 't want t r eatment. In fact, they enjoy exposing themselves. And accord − ing to the literature and their previous therapists, the prognoses are terrible. Should I refer them to someone else who knows how to handle this?"

Our fears cause us to forget our own competencies and view the new client as a label we have never encountered before:

"an anorexic," "a manic-depressive," "a borderline ." The labels can generate fear, anxiety, and self-doubt. And yet when the client sits before us, and we see not the diagnosis but the unique individual, our fears subside and our confidence and skills return.

But of course we have lived through these self-doubts be - fore —the first time we dealt with someone who was suicidal or hallucinating, for example, or the first client with an incurable disease or a mean disposition. We resolve this particular crisis, at least for a little while, upon reflecting that we do not have to know everything that is going on as long as we are determined t o find out the answers. In other words, we recall the number of similar instances when we did not know exactly what to do but were able to stretch ourselves, expand our resources, and work things out. Otherwise, we would end up referring every new client who walks through the door instead of just those who ex - hibit symptoms considerably beyond our expertise or those who are not compatible with our style.

What I f M y Treatment Harms a Client? When and when not to delve into the unknown leads us to the third stage—the fear of hurting a client through our neglect or incompetence. This is, of course, a healthy fear since it keeps us appropriately respect- ful of our potential to do harm as well as good. Yet this fear of failure can become debilitating for those who are constantly censoring themselves with admonishments, believing they will surely say or do the "wrong " thing and inadvertently cause someone to kill themselves or have a breakdown.

In a training group of beginning therapists that I (J.K .) have been leading for some time, there is a marked reluctance among the participants to risk trying any but the most benign i nterventions. The interactions are brimming with goodwill-supportive comments, caring reflections of feeling, safe inter- pretations. But there is a significant absence of any confronta - t i on whatsoever—a strange occurrence in a group that has met for almost a year. Finally, one of the participants confided her frustration. She had observed very few conflicts during the life of the group, had seen almost no expressions of anger, and had noticed that members seemed unwilling to confront one another about obviously dysfunctional behavior. Why were they so un − willing to be more direct with one another, more honest and authentic in their encounters?

Most of these beginning therapists said they were not confrontive with one another because they did not want to hurt anybody. Better, they justified, to let someone ramble inces− santly or contradict themselves rather than risk hurting their feelings. Typical of the inexperienced, they feared that a single badly timed intervention or awkwardly worded confrontation would destroy the client. Not only in their training group, but at their internship sites, they were inclined to do little else than listen attentively and offer a bit of encouragement. This helping style, of course, matures with greater experience and confidence.

After many years we eventually learn that there is a lot of l atitude in what constitutes effective therapy or a "correct" in− t ervention. We learn that clients are more resilient than we t hought—that it takes more than a mistimed interpretation or a fumbling gesture to destroy a client's world. We realize they do not listen that closely to the content of what we say, anyway, as much as sense our genuine caring for their well-being. Neverthe− less, the concern with hurting a client never goes away —as well it s hould not.

It is this apprehension that helps to separate the ignorant from the wise. In discussing the dangers of not acknowledging our limitations, Hoff (1982, p. 44) draws an excerpt from **Win− nie the Pooh.** Tigger is bragging to Roo about how wonderful his species is, how Tiggers can do almost anything. Roo defiant− ly asks if his kind can fly.

"Yes," said Tigger, "they 're very good flyers, Tiggers are, Storny good flyers."

"Oo ! " said Roo. "Can they fly as well as Owls?"

"Yes," said Tigger. "Only they don 't want to ."

It is ironic that acknowledging our imperfections—admit− ti ng this very fear of doing damage—is what distinguishes the competent from less conscientious colleagues who never consider t hat they may be doing harm . The defense mechanisms of some practitioners prevent them from consulting their conscience and acknowledging their inner doubts. They would rarely admit to feeling less than absolutely certain about their actions, and they might disdain those who do reveal their uncertainties. In the words of one psychiatrist: "We ought not to be concerned about those therapists who don 't think they know what they 're doing; rather, we should worry about those who think they do " (Williams, personal communication , 1984).

What I f I 'm Caught Making a Mistake? As experience broadens, so does experimentation in methods and subsequent risks. We develop a looser, more flexible style of practice. We may also become more prosperous and prominent in the community , more concerned with our reputation . Stage four is the fear of getting caught making a mistake.

When a client overreacts to a disappointment in life by personalizing its significance beyond what is considered reasonable, it is called "narcissistic loss." There is an overinvestment in one 's image and the way things might appear to others. Lowen (1983) goes on to describe other qualities of narcissistic charact er structures that sound hauntingly familiar among our own ranks—a denial of feeling protected by a need for control in relationships, doing good for others as a means of winning power and indebtedness, arrogance of the ego, exaggerated displays of self-confidence, dignity, and superiority. While this portrait may not describe us, it certainly portrays others we might know in t he field. And because we are all prone to narcissistic loss, we are especially harsh critics of our own behavior. We cannot afford to make a serious mistake for fear it would be publicly displayed. It is not only a concern for appearances, however, but a legitimate worry that a single error could destroy a career. Who among us does not tremble at the thought that a disgruntled client might some day call a press conference to accuse us of some great or small misjudgment? Each day 's mail could bring a censure from the Licensing Board or an inquiry from the Ethics Committee regarding some real or imagined transgression.

We even fear that we may one day cross the line and lose control of ourselves. This nightmare could take different forms—

"catching " the client's symptoms and going mad, letting oneself be seduced by a client, becoming inappropriately intimate, losing one 's temper in a fit of rage. In all its manifestations the fear of failing through loss of self-control is particularly devastating t o contemplate since it involves a threat to that which we hold most sacred. The frightening thing about impulses is that they seem to come out of nowhere without warning. Nobody, no matter how controlled, is immune from the pull of an irrational impulse. One need not be a psychopathic personality, an im − moral creature, to give in to an inner push that defies reasoning.

Sometimes we may feel like punching a client's abusive parent. Sometimes we feel like screaming in frustration with a client who is stubborn . And sometimes, just for an instant or t wo, we feel an irresistible compulsion to embrace an attractive client. Yes, yes, we know. All of these things are wrong. We would never actually do them . But somebody , who once thought very much like we do, did. We could be thoroughly competent and ethical every day of our professional lives and then, one day very much like all the others, in a session not particularly un − usual, with a client not all that distinctive from the rest, we might lose complete control. One minute we are cruising along and the next we find ourselves already remorseful about some action committed by somebody else using our body. It probably would not happen. But it might.

One especially even-tempered psychiatrist, who had been practicing intensive psychoanalytic treatment with a stubborn adolescent for about a year, completely lost control one day. He went into a rage of anger and frustration . He felt manipulated . He expressed his fury in no uncertain terms, using all of his acumen to cut this arrogant, manipulative kid down to size. Once t he client stormed out of the office, the psychiatrist was filled with remorse. He tried on several occasions to call and apologize, but the damage was done. And he felt just as distraught by the prospect that he carried around within him such explosive anger as he was worried about the disastrous loss of a client, who now felt humiliated and turned off to the prospect of ever trusting a t herapist again.

It is only through continued supervision and personal

t herapy that we can temper these fears and hope to continue close therapeutic relationships without being afraid of lapses i nto self-indulgence. But no matter how much work we do on ourselves to analyze our neurotic urges, there is always some remnant of our impulsivity left untouched .

No matter how successful your career is or how esteemed you are by your colleagues, all it takes is a single lapse to end up in court defending your integrity. This is no paranoid delusion or exaggeration of risk. Just underestimate the power of a bor‑ derline personality or the suicidal risk of a distraught child and watch your world come tumbling down. Alienate an angry spouse, confront somebody too vigorously, forget to leave an emergency number with the answering service, write a sloppy t r eatment plan or a psychological report that is too candid, and you could quite conceivably be facing a lawsuit.

Many of us are attracted to treatment approaches that en ‑ courage a relatively passive therapist role because, by doing less, we minimize the risk of having some interventions backfire. Re‑ flections of feeling, mild interpretations, silence, and verbal acknowledgments are less intrusive, dramatic, and dangerous t han confrontation , goal setting, or paradoxical directives. Even t hough the likelihood of doing damage is greater with these more active responses, treatment is usually shorter. Ideally the client, as an informed consumer, decides whether he or she pre‑ fers a safe therapy that takes longer or a confrontational style t hat produces quicker results with more risk. Although we at‑ t empt to keep the risks under control by defensive documenta ‑ t i on, conservative practice, and carefully monitoring our emo ‑ t i onal responses, our underlying commitment to our client's growth constantly challenges us to take steps into the unknown . At times we must simply accept our imperfections and trust t hat we are doing the best we can.

What I f I'm N ot Really Doing Anything ?

The fifth fear of fail‑ ure is almost the reverse of the previous concern that we might injure someone by trying to do too much —in this case, we fear t hat we are not really doing anything at all. Although we are constantly explaining why we believe therapy works, during moments of painful honesty we recognize that we really do not understand very well how people alter their behavior as a result of talking to us.

When a patient complains of constant fatigue and short‐ness of breath, the physician can fairly reliably diagnose a faulty mitral valve by listening to the heart 's low -pitched murmur and t hen confirming the impression with an echocardiogram . The surgeon can then go into the chest, open up the heart, take out t he calcified valve, and replace it with a Teflon model. Both doctor and patient can then breathe easier, secure in the knowl‐edge that the problem has been resolved. Human behavior, how ‐ever, is much too complex for even experts to comprehend fully. Even after the client has left treatment, restored to inner peace, we do not know what exactly happened . Whereas the physician can examine the broken mitral valve to confirm that it was in‐deed causing the discomfort, there is no comparable test we can perform to find out what went wrong and how we fixed it.

Even a relatively straightforward case of depressive ad‐j ustment reaction to divorce can turn out to be deceptively complex. We may treat that condition, focusing on the client's loss of self-esteem, adjustment to single life, anger toward the ex-spouse, yet never learn why the client actually improved. Perhaps there was some hormonal or neurological imbalance t hat coincided with the marital breakup. Maybe it was not our planned interventions that made a difference, but something we said or did spontaneously that nobody remembers. In convers‐ing with clients who have successfully completed therapy, it never ceases to amaze us when they tell us the actions they be‐lieve made a difference. Years or even decades later, a client will quote some passing remark that changed everything—a remark we may not even remember!

Since we do not really know what is going on most of the time, we advance at a cautious pace. Listen a lot. Ask a few questions. Pause a bit to give the client (and ourselves) a chance t o figure out where to go next. Urge the client to continue talk‐ ing. Nod. "You feeling any better yet ? " Then wait a spell and see what comes up next.

No matter how prominent we may become, how stable

and secure, there is always the possibility that new clients will stop coming, current clients will cease their progress, and our practice will inexplicably die. What if the referrals stop? Such t hings do happen. A therapist suddenly gets tired of listening to herself repeat the same observations. She feels exhausted and stale. She stops believing in the power of her promises. She is ti red of persuading people to stop pouting , cease hurting them - selves, to grow up, take risks, make decisions. She feels like an accomplished actor who repeats her lines, performance after performance, for an audience of one. With diminished convic- t i on, her soliloquies that once seemed so powerful now sound as i f t hey were read in a monotone by a listless ninth grader. Since she believes she has heard it all before, she no longer listens very closely to what her clients say. It 's the same old stuff anyway. Whining. Complaining. Excuses.

While this could indeed happen , it is pretty unlikely. We soon discover the ebb and flow of our work —challenged when our time is demanded and overscheduled, relieved when there is a temporary lull. We come to realize that our referrals, just like everything else in the universe, have a natural rhythm of in- crease and decrease over time.

Our rational voice can remind us again and again that no - body can ever take away what we already know. While time may erode our memories, this aging effect is counteracted by t he gain in experience and wisdom . Yet when we have devoted a li fetime to study and growth it becomes our most valued com - modity. In nightmares or periods of despair, our defenses are down and we fear losing that which we value the most: our power to heal. There is an inexplicable magic associated with our presence, our voice, our intuition. What if one day we wake up and no longer entertain any profound thoughts? What if peo - ple stop laughing at our jokes? What if we simply cease feeling sensitive to others?

Our feelings of imposture and fraud resolve, however, with the startling insight that even if it were true that we are only a compassionate friend who is paid by the hour, where else would the client find such a person? We realize there is nothing more difficult and exhausting —for any amount of money —than t o be a truly helpful listener. And who says that doing some− t hing else (surgery, for example) is more beneficial than simply facilitating the natural cure of the human spirit?

What If M y Life 's Work Really Doesn't Matter? Inevitably, at

some time or another, every clinician becomes disenchanted, bored, burned out. To the experienced therapist comes a pain− ful recognition that some clients cannot reshape their lives de − spite the clinician's extensive knowledge, experience, and com − mitment. The angst that led us to choose the therapist's path in t he first place rekindles the fear that after a lifetime devoted to helping, we never made a difference. To the impersonal eye of t he universe, nothing we ever did really mattered.

We reflect upon those lives we have touched and wonder if we really had an impact. This is the sixth stage of fear of failure. Perhaps what used to be of such concern now seems dull and unimportant. Not knowing how the clients in whom we in− vested so much energy and hope are currently functioning con − t r i butes to this doubt and wondering. Clients returning with the same patterns give us pause. As we gain more experience, our perspectives are altered, our values shift, our expectations change. We look through a larger lens at the many clients who have crossed our threshold and we wonder. This self-doubt may bring about shifts in our work, a reemphasis on key themes, a letting go of others, a rededication to a continued search for meaning in our lives. Anderson (1 9 8 7) confirms that at this midlife period in her professional development, her mastery of the field freed her to reexamine her values, priorities, and frame of reference, enabling her ultimately to come to terms with her strengths and, more important, her limitations.

While concern about the meaning of our work stirs our consciousness and, at times, questions of failure shake the very foundation of our existence, eventually a client appears who again captures our curiosity, stimulates and challenges our re− sources, and, in generating sparks of renewed energy and rekin− dled spirit, reminds us, once again, that what we do is indeed worthwhile.

Recently a client ended therapy whom I (D.B.) had seen regularly over a six-month period of weekly sessions. We had worked on self-esteem issues and addressed some marital and parenting problems that to me seemed rather straightforward. As she took leave, the client enumerated significant gains, em - braced me in tears, and passionately expressed how much ther- apy had meant to her. With all of my great expectations, I had neglected to consider the experience from her perspective. What had become run of the mill to me had been of utmost signifi- cance to her.

A Framework for Understanding. These six questions provide a framework for understanding how we view ourselves and our work during our professional lives, what we need to confront and come to terms with —and how easy it is to avoid self-con- frontation . For these are frightening questions that expose our deepest fears. The preceding description of the role that failure plays in the development of a therapist helps explain why the subject is so assiduously avoided. Not only on the playing field or in the locker room are we reluctant to consider our errors, but even in the privacy of our minds we deceive ourselves.

There is something to be said for ignorant bliss. By avoid- ing a confrontation with failure, we protect our ego and insecuri- ties. We prevent paralysis of will after discovering how primitive are our theories and inefficient are our interventions. We en - hance our power as models by minimizing imperfections and cultivating an image of omnipotence. Avoiding thoughts of fail- ure allows us to preserve our inflated sense of hope —which most certainly has a positive effect on the client's belief system . By not considering the possibilities of failure we can concentrate more intently on success.

Keeping Failure at a Distance

In many martial arts one primary strategy of defense is to use your opponent 's force against him. This is best accomplished by memorizing a series of actions that become embedded in the reflexes through repetition. If you can master simple parries, subtle movements, and weight shifts to avoid a strike, your op - ponent finds himself kicking air, unnerved, off balance.

Therapists use many ingenious methods to avoid the idea

of failure even if we cannot stave off its inevitability in practice. We try to fool ourselves in a host of ways. Perhaps the most common ploy is the government's propaganda strategy during t h e Vietnam War—no matter how badly you are losing the war, pretend you are winning. If you cannot justify continued ex - penditures of time and resources based on body counts as a measure of success, try another dependent variable—square miles of foliage napalmed to ashes. While pretending that things are proceeding much better than they appear, therapists follow sev - eral guidelines that parallel those of the military high command :

- No matter how bleak the situation looks, keep smiling and act as if everything is under control.
- When asked whether things are indeed deteriorating, formu - late a response that implies the question is absolutely ludi - crous.
- If you are caught squarely in a lie or deception , blame fac - t ors out of your control   (the client's pathology, the lighting in the room).
- Rephrase defeats in more positive terms —just as a retreat be - comes a "strategic withdrawal," a psychotic episode becomes a "temporary withdrawal."
- Provide a disclaimer or predict a relapse before attempting an intervention that might not work.
- If in spite of your best efforts the client still refuses to coop - erate and make a miraculous recovery, insist that he was not **ready** to change.

Many clients recognize the advantages of avoiding respon - sibility for their plight. It is not their fault they are unhappy ; God, bad genes, an unhappy childhood, improper toilet train - ing, bad luck, Mom , or "someone who has it in for m e " is the cause of their suffering. Therapists, as well, are quite skilled at finding reasonable explanations why things have gone awry. Here are some common ways in which we externalize blame:

- "You 're not really trying ."
- "You 're trying too hard ."
- "You only think you 're trying ."

- "When I told you . . . , I didn 't know that.   ."
- "There must be something you 're not telling me ."

If a client attacks our integrity or competence , there are a num − ber of effective ripostes:

- "The reason the therapy hasn 't worked is that you 're threat− ened by the consequences of having to change."
- "Even though, on the surface, you appear to be very cooper− ative in your treatment, you 're actually sabotaging your progress."
- "You haven 't given us enough time ."
- "This is all part of the transference ."
- "This is all part of your unusual pattern of denial and defen − siveness."
- "What do you mean the therapy isn't working? Of course it is working! If it wasn 't, you wouldn 't have the courage to confront me on this very issue."

These defenses are hard to deny, even harder to prove. Nevertheless, they serve their purpose of leaving the therapist relatively blameless and unscathed. In his parody of therapists who are terrified of appearing incompetent, Haley (1980) sug− gests that the best strategy of all is to do as little as possible dur− ing sessions: If you do not say much, you will not be contra − dicted later. If you insist on intervening in some way, pretend t hat the outcome is exactly what you originally intended.

While the preceding ploys to deal with failure were pre− sented tongue in cheek, we may still recognize ourselves, at one t i me or another, as having uttered similar phrases. In a more serious vein, we may also see ourselves in the following descrip− t i ons offered by Martin and Schurtman (1985). Here are some of the defensive maneuvers therapists use to deal with their anxieties surrounding premature termination and to avoid con− fronting failure:

- **Reversal o f affect.** In this form of reaction formation , the

    t herapist masks feelings of anger, rejection, and frustration with a shallow resignation of the situation. The client is rare−

ly fooled by the pretense and often will leave with lingering guilt and uncertainty about the decision. "Perhaps it is best t hatyou leave. You 're right—we don 't have much else to do . "

• **Projection.** The therapist converts his feelings of abandon ment into an aggressive stance in which confrontation is used as an excuse to be punitive. On a more subtle level, the ther apist may withdraw and adapt an aloof posture both to pro t ect himself from rejection and to repay the hurt. "How do I feel about your decision not to come back? I think you 're j ust running away from your problems. But frankly, I don 't have any open time slots anyway . "

• **Principalization.** The therapist uses intellectualization to dis t ance herself from the pain of separation and failure. She may appeal to some general principle of practice to deny the i ntensity of personal feelings. "This is a good opportunity for you to end a relationship with responsibility and maturity . "

• **Turning against the self.** If the therapist feels wounded , ne gated, and diminished, he may panic and turn his anger in ward. Self-blame, self-doubt, self-deprecation are common . In a last-ditch effort to redeem himself, the therapist may work extra hard to try to salvage some piece of learning for t he client. "Well, you must have gotten **something** out of t hese sessions?"

• **Turning against the other.** In the most direct and aggressive of defensive responses, the therapist may try to provoke the client in some way. Sometimes this anger can be displaced to a member of the client's family. "I understand this must be difficult for you. But, hey, when your husband issues an order, you salute."

Defining Goals (or Not)

Therapists who are not strictly behavioral in their orien t ation tend to be evasive when asked what is likely to happen in t r eatment and how long it will take. Sometimes this cloak of secrecy comes from our preference to withhold predictions or j udgments until we have a feel for the client, the situation, and what is disturbing him. But another part of this close-mouthed strategy stems from a reluctance to be held accountable for t hings we cannot control.

Once we have declared what we think will occur and how l ong it will probably take, the client will fully expect these predictions to become fact. In a sense, once committed to a specific path, the therapist cannot win. If things go just as predicted, the client will feel modestly satisfied—after all, that is exactly the product that was paid for. Further, the client will come to expect such precise results for every problem in the future. And why not? If I am experiencing sleeplessness, agitat i on, and a restless spirit, I consult the professional who gives this condition a name, tells me what I must do, and when 1 can expect to feel better. If this outcome does in fact occur, I am going to expect similar results the next time I consult a therapist for problems with my spouse or kids or job or sense of futility with my life. And woe to the person who cannot deliver me from anguish a second, third, and fourth time.

If, on the other hand, things take longer (or even shorter) t han predicted, clients may begin to lose faith in our expertise. They may feel betrayed , cheated, misled. They may think of us as frauds and demand retribution . Better, we reason, to avoid this whole irate business by promising very little. And so we avoid failure by refusing to define, for each case, what specifically constitutes success. We might not be able to guarantee that t he symptoms will completely disappear, but we can offer assurances that the client will understand where they may have come from and what functions they probably serve. We can even help the person to pay less attention to the disturbance, even if we cannot make it go away.

One therapist had been practicing for years a kind of dy - namic, insight-oriented, existential therapy with modest and consistent results. In six months, a year, or two, the vast maj ority of his clients would leave treatment more self-aware, feeling better, and acting more effectively in their lives. Perhaps one in ten would not improve much at all, even after years of treatment, but since no goals were ever explicitly stated, these clients might quietly drift out of treatment. Or then again, some would stay indefinitely, content with weekly contact with a caring listener.

This therapist, like many others, wondered if he might improve his satisfactory "cure rate" by augmenting his therapeutic style with one of the new techniques in vogue. Hypnosis was the current favorite, and many practitioners were flocking to workshops for training in this mysterious but apparently helpful intervention. The therapist studied and practiced hard with his new tool and began to integrate hypnotic procedures into his work, hoping to help his clients gain greater behavioral control over symptoms that seemed impervious to his usual therapeutic regimen. He wondered if he might help some of his clients lose weight or stop smoking, for example, and found to his surprise that indeed more than two-thirds of the people he worked with felt newfound control in their lives. Yet he felt little satisfaction from these many clients who were elated by a smoke-free or fat-free life. It was instead on the one-third who did not improve that he focused his attention.

Since there were but two possibilities—people either lost weight or they did not, they either stopped smoking or continued their habit—it was readily apparent when the induction procedure failed. Much to his consternation, the therapist experienced the wrath of the clients who clearly had not improved. They became indignant. They confirmed his worst fears that he was a fraud. Some demanded their money back. One particularly disappointed woman even threatened to file a lawsuit against him.

Even though he guaranteed no cures, it was easy for clients to measure his success or failure. So he tried interpretation and reframing interventions to soften the blows of disappointment and disown responsibility for the failure: "I guess you're not ready to change yet" or "Just because the hypnotic suggestion hasn't worked doesn't mean it isn't fermenting inside you. It will only become an active force when the time is right." Then the therapist began to hedge his language during hypnotic suggestions: "When you are ready, you will begin to notice fewer cravings for . . ." Eventually, however, he dropped the use of these techniques completely. He just could not live with the consequences of practicing his profession in such a way t hat his failures were so apparent. He preferred instead the cus- t omary hues of gray rather than black and white. In the former world to which he had become accustomed, people only ap - peared to get better or worse. Since no one could ever be cer- t ain exactly what was transpiring, he rarely had to deal with t he experience of failing.

A client who terminates treatment prematurely may be doing so precisely because it was working too well. The authors of one study on premature termination in therapy offered the following explanation: "It appears that involvement with the t herapist, even in an aborted therapy, is productive to the well- being of the patient. Perhaps therapists ought not to consider patient termination as much of a failure when the cause of ter- mination is related to their interaction with the patient" (Levin- son, McMurray, Podell, and Weiner, 1978, p. 829).

The client complaining of minimal relief may not be giv- ing the effects of therapy enough time —sometimes it takes years for a realization to sink in. The truth is: If we are reasonably cautious to speak in generalities ("Many people find . . . "), promise very little ("I can't say for certain"), evade direct ques- t i ons ("What do you think?"), and avoid clearly defined goals ("Let's wait and see what unfolds"), we can avoid the label of failure altogether. Instead, every outcome can be viewed on a relative continuum of success. Of course, by adopting such an ambiguous stance, we may prevent the client from establishing challenging goals.

And so we feed our egos and protect ourselves from expe- riencing failure and continue to perpetuate the myth in our pro - fession that if failure occurs, it is them not us. If our own falli- bility is suspect, no one need know, least of all ourselves. In the next chapter we examine in greater detail the specific ways in which therapists try to keep failure at bay.

3

Unproductive   Defenses
Against Failure

No matter how hard we may try to avoid dealing with failure, complete escape is impossible. It permeates our waking mo -
ments and creeps into our dreams. Yet many of us go to extra-
ordinary7 lengths to distance ourselves from our imperfections.
We deny their existence and disguise their presence in other
forms. We medicate the pain away. We develop detached or self-
protective attitudes. We isolate ourselves from possible criticism.
We overwork and overwhelm ourselves to the point where there
is little time to reflect on what went wrong. But ultimately these
defenses are no more successful than those our clients bring to
t heir sessions.

The Doctor Who Refused to Fail

A woman had been in treatment with a psychiatric resident for seven months. The psychiatrist, a woman of East Indian
descent, had struggled throughout her medical career against the
prejudices formulated by her male colleagues and supervisors.
She was used to working harder than anyone else and developed
a tenacious spirit toward any challenge. The patient had been
experiencing panic attacks, generalized anxiety, sleeplessness,
and recently, because her symptoms were getting worse, she was
becoming increasingly despondent and frustrated. The doctor
had been seeing her in individual therapy two or three times a
week for the past seven months, yet the patient's symptoms resisted every effort on the young psychiatrist's part to alter them .
Since it was apparent that therapy sessions consisting
mostly of nondirective listening were not of much use, the doc -

t or renewed her determination to conquer this case. She pre-scribed a variety of anti-anxiety and tranquilizing agents, but t hey too proved ineffective. As the patient became increasingly frustrated and anxious, so did her doctor. But the psychiatrist refused to give up the case or even to seek consultation, which she believed would show weakness on her part. She was certain, given enough time, that things could be worked out.

By this time, however, the patient was extremely frus t r ated and angry. When a friend suggested she consult another professional for a second opinion , she jum ped at the opportu nity—" After all, seven m onths is surely enough time to give her, isn't it ? I mean, she's a nice doctor and all, and she's been trying so hard to help me, but I haven't improved much and I still don't understand what this is all about. In this one session you explained to me more than she has in seven months. And the relaxation exercise you just showed me has already helped me to calm down. I'll talk to her and see what she says."

After this consultation with another therapist, the patient returned to the psychiatrist to tie up loose ends and explain t hat she would not be returning. Although the psychiatrist had by now completed her residency and was driving all the way across town for this single patient, she felt no relief at the pros- pect of losing the case. After listening to the patient relate the details of her other session and plead that because of financial pressures she would be unable to return, the doctor offered to reduce her fee to five dollars.

The patient called back the other therapist to pass on her decision—" Look, you really helped me and gave me hope. I would like to work with you , but I don 't think she will ever let me go. And I would feel too bad if I just left her. I know she hasn 't helped me, but she keeps telling me to give her more ti me ."

In her desperation to avoid failure, the psychiatrist refused t o let go of her patient. She was unwilling to acknowledge her fallibility despite the client's suffering. As long as the client kept coming back, there was still a chance that success could be achieved. By tenaciously holding on to this belief, the psychi-atrist kept the shadows of failure away.

Disowning Failure

From a poll we conducted of prominent theoreticians, as well as conversations with several hundred professionals, it is apparent that not all therapists experience failure. Whether this is because some practitioners have attained perfection in their work, or simply believe they have, is a matter for conjecture. In either case, failure does not appear to exist for these few. Indeed, one of them responded with indignation to our invitation t o contribute an example of imperfection.

We ran across several others who, by their own terms, do not fail—not because they believe themselves to be perfect, but because they do not subscribe to the concept of judgment. They do not see the value in utilizing a success/failure continuum and, instead, prefer to suspend all evaluative processes from t heir minds while engaged with the client. Perhaps this absence of "How am I doing ? " facilitates more effective listening to and focusing on the problem at hand. Although we find it difficult t o imagine how a therapist could ever completely avoid evaluative thinking, especially because we are constantly making judg - ments regarding people 's behavior even if we totally accept t hem as human beings, we see definite merit in this stance. It is certainly a desirable goal to transcend, as much as possible, the tendency to compare ourselves to some absolute stan - dard.

But failure is inevitable when one is dealing with repeti- ti ve actions, so any attempt to disown it will also fail. There are, then, those who make mistakes they refuse to acknowledge, who lose clients they claim to have cured, and who pretend a perfection they cannot demonstrate. Perhaps all of us are guilty, t o some extent, of these signs of omission. That is, we fail to mention that:

* Although the client feels immensely grateful to us for all we have done, such excessive homage is the result of promoting t oo much dependency in the relationship.
* Although we were absolutely correct in our prediction of what would occur, we missed a lot of cues that could have i ndicated otherwise.

- Although the client left a satisfied customer, she is still engaging in the same dysfunctional behavior.
- Although the divorce is probably for the better, marital therapy might have worked had we been able to establish a working alliance with the spouse.
- Although it looks as if the client has worked through the t r auma, it was our own fear that inhibited the process.
- Although the client improved markedly in just a few sessions, his progress had less to do with our efforts than with his child 's health improving.
- Although anyone might have done what we did in the situati on, we were still wrong.

Failure stimulates further failure when a person stubborn - ly refuses to acknowledge negative outcomes. A character from a novel by Conroy (1986) comments on his father 's repeatedly unsuccessful business enterprises: "He never learned a single thing from his mistakes. Each failure, and there were dozens of them , only served to convince him that his time was approaching and that his apprenticeship in the harsh milieu of commerce was nearing its end. All he lacked was luck, he told us again and again" (p. 243). A therapist who never fails must feel incredible pressure to maintain a perfect record. Each case must be chosen carefully; those with poor prognoses must be referred elsewhere. Since mistakes or miscalculations cannot be risked, only the most reliable interventions can be used; any strategy remotely creative or experimental must be avoided. Each and every' session becomes a test of one 's competence and sterling reputation . And the slightest lapse must be covered up.

Therapists who do not fail are often threatened by clients who do. After investing so much energy in the pursuit of perfec- t i on, the flawless therapist's personal value system must empha - size success above all else. Since most clients come to therapy at a time in their lives when they hardly feel successful, there is a vast schism of experience between the two parties. Whereas the client feels insecure, lacks confidence, and struggles with a pervasive sense of failure, the therapist exudes confidence and success. If ever people were unlikely to meet on common ground as equals, it would be these two. In this relationship there is no doubt whatsoever who is in control and who is not. Whether the client could ever recover from this one-down position, feel inspired by the obviously successful model, and work his way out of the hole would depend very much on how the therapist han – dles the situation. But when the helper communicates in such certain terms that success is all-important, a client cannot help but feel intimidated.

Effects of Unsuccessful Attempts to Deal with Failure

Therapists who do not acknowledge their mistakes are doomed to repeat them . Their growth is stunted as they are un – able or unwilling to recognize their deficiencies and realize their weaknesses. If they should lose a client through some miscalcu– l ation or error in judgment, they would fail to concede their role in the disaster. The very next time a similar situation arose, t hey would, more than likely, inadvertently repeat their mis– t akes without realizing it.

To improve one 's performance, whatever the activity, re– quires that one become aware of the impact each action has on t he probability of reaching a desired goal. In the case of tennis, for example, if you simply swing the racket and ignore the dif– ferences in technique that produce won and lost points, there is no way you can ever improve. In an activity even more complex such as the practice of therapy, honest self-assessment is even more crucial to continued growth.

Another result of the therapist's effort to deny failure is t he development of blind spots. One 's conflicts are repressed and one 's apprehensions go underground , cropping up in vari– ous forms of counter-transference that sabotage treatment. Clients suffer not only from their therapist's stagnation, but also from his neurotic lapses. There is nothing more dangerous than a wounded healer who thinks he is in perfect working order.

Ellis (1985) suggests that some of the same irrational be – liefs adopted by clients operate in therapists to create blind spots, unrealistic expectations, unnecessary internal pressure, and sabotage efforts at treatment. The following statements are commonly associated with failure:

- "I have to be successful with all my clients."
- "If things don't work out the way the client would prefer, it's my fault."
- "I must always be accurate in my diagnoses and interpreta-tions."
- "Because I'm a therapist, I should have no emotional prob-lems myself."
- "All my clients must love me and feel grateful for my ef-forts."
- "My clients should be as responsible, motivated, and hard-working as I am in overcoming conflict."
- "My clients should listen to me, cooperate with my sugges-tions, and not be resistant."
- "Progress in therapy should proceed smoothly and easily."
- "I should be aware of all my irrational beliefs and blind spots, and be able to keep them under control."

Goleman (1 9 8 5) writes of the blind spots we all develop in order to diminish anxiety. Alone, and in collusion with oth - ers, we perpetuate illusion and agree to ignore that which is painful. The most destructive scenario is thus one in which we continue to live in a fictitious world of our own making. We see what we choose to see and deny or distort anything that does not fit our achievement-oriented script. The more our success is t hreatened , the more rigidly we clasp our protective shield. Fi- nally, we withdraw from others whose statements challenge the image we have resolved to protect.

Scott (1982) describes such persons as becoming so en - t r enched in their own self-definitions that they guard against any information that threatens this fixed view and thus are "un - prepared to face the enormous range of opposites and differ-ences that make up being human . . When I am opposed to the eventfulness of my own being, I will be predisposed to blocking openness and pervasiveness at all points in my existence. I will want to control my bowels as well as my children. I will feel the t hreat of merger and loss of identity in all dimensions of relat- ing with others that do not involve clarity of intention and a sense of control" (p. 68).

Clients take their cues from us. Our discomfort increases t heir uncertainty ; our unrealistic demands only exacerbate their frustration and anxiety. Safety and trust become diminished and central issues go unattended . When the emotional tempera - t ure gets too high, for example, we try to turn it down without even knowing we are inhibiting our clients from deeper self- exploration. If we have trouble with our own anger, we may in- advertently repress it in our clients. Our fear of loss may sup- press their expression of sadness. We hasten to offer Kleenex so they can quickly dry their eyes—and so we ourselves will not betray our own grief. But if we are unwilling to see the subtle l i mitations we may be placing on our clients and refuse to look inward, a cycle of rigidity and stagnation becomes perpetuated . In our compulsion to keep emotionally afloat, we unwittingly prevent our clients from making any waves that might upset this fragile balance.

Rigidity and Burnout. This great reluctance of many therapists

t o admit defeat appears at first like a successful strategy for dealing with failure. After all, those who can hide behind the protective tenets of their theory are impermeable to criticism, disappointment, or defeat. Such clinicians can interpret a cli- ent 's unpredictable actions as "resistance" and can regard re- j ected interventions as "defense mechanisms." They can reframe premature termination as a "flight to health " or hostility as "transference." The only way failure could ever occur with such practitioners is if they were to depart from their rigid rules and roles.

Yet the common prescription of rigidity and denial to combat potential confrontations with failure has its side effects. In a study of rigidity among psychodynamic therapists, Heil- man, Morrison, and Abramowitz (1987) discovered that those prone to dogmatism , fusion with the social environment, intol- erance of ambiguity, and habitual rigidity reported greater levels of stress in their lives than their more flexible colleagues. It would appear, then, that the degree of intolerance implicit in a t herapist's style predisposes him or her to greater vulnerability t o personal stress and to negative effects from being exposed to t heir clients' suicidal threats, resistance, and psychopathological symptoms.

The researchers draw implications about the propensity for some therapists to develop burnout. Personal rigidity not only makes therapists more vulnerable to stress, but it is associated with increased frustration and demoralization that others such as Farber (1 9 8 3) and Maslach (1 9 8 2) believe may intensify burnout effects. Among the sources of stress that lead to burn - out, Deutsch (1984) found that therapists who subscribed to t he irrational beliefs mentioned earlier—such as "I must be successful with all my clients" —were most susceptible to stress-induced burnout. In fact, of the 264 practitioners who de - scribed their worst experiences in the field, the vast majority of cases involved flirtations with failure.

Burnout reflects a closed system in which few options are seen. The exchange of information is restricted; little goes out, less comes in. Rigidity sets in, offering an illusion of safety and predictability. As therapists experience failure and disappoint- ment, and become dispirited when their expectations are un - met, they withdraw further into a locked system characterized by repetition and depersonalization. Whatever threatens their security is resisted; boredom and cynicism flourish in this atmo - sphere. At its most insidious, burnout produces a dulled lethargy, inattentiveness, even a lifeless human being.

Fine (1980) writes of the midlife despair that so com - monly occurs in the life of a therapist. After attaining a degree of success, productivity, and proficiency at the craft, many practitioners experience an erosion of will. Certain other symp - t oms become evident—increased cynicism about the field and greater appreciation for irony, repeated skirmishes with col- leagues, feeling bored with long-term cases and wishing im - patiently to terminate them , general feelings of fatigue, empti- ness, and depression. In the depleted spirit of the burned -out t herapist, pessimism, detachment, disengagement, and self- doubt become pervasive. "For it was the dying Socrates who warned that there is no greater danger than to suffer intellectual failure and to put the blame not on oneself, not on one 's inabil- i t y to think properly, but on thought itself, to cast doubt and even to repudiate one 's capacity and one 's duty to think " (Fine, 1980, p. 395).

With this outlook , of course, failure can run rampant. Closed to risk, to improvisation, to creativity, the therapist dog‐ gedly adheres to a narrow scope of practice. Threatened by change, he or she sticks persistently with the predictable. In‐ attentiveness leads to missed cues; overcompensation may re‐ sult. The therapeutic process becomes skewed and the therapist becomes ever more desperate for control. But the need for greater control merely increases the therapist's rigidity, which, in turn, accelerates the same deadly cycle: Burnout is height‐ ened and failure, rather than being avoided, becomes a certainty.

Isolation. The single most unsuccessful strategy used to avoid or deny failure, the one with the most devastating effects, is when t he client or therapist attempts to isolate himself. While it may appear that separating oneself from others, becoming aloof, in‐ different to others ' opinions, is an excellent way to free oneself from the pressures of critical judgments, such a tactic only simulates the worst effects of the condition one wishes to avoid. For failure represents a retreat into loneliness, a flight from inti‐ macy, and a denial of self.

People who choose a solitary existence answer only to themselves for their actions. They are immune from others ' as‐ sessment of their performance and exercise maximum control over the daily circumstances of life. Such isolation permits ther‐ apists to draw their own conclusions regarding how things are going without interference from others. Even the client's dissat‐ i sfaction with treatment can be explained away when there is nobody else to appease.

We are not referring here to one 's office arrangement— t hat is, whether one works alone in a single office or with many partners. Rather, we are discussing the way a therapist struc‐ t ures his or her professional life. Some practitioners work in the company of a crowd but disdain supervision, refuse to consult colleagues when they get stuck, and reject personal therapy for themselves when they feel the need. And there are solitary prac‐ t i t i o ners who have created an elaborate social and professional network for getting others ' opinions on cases as well as emo ‑ t i onal support.

There are many reasons why isolation does not work for a therapist hiding from failure. We know from exposure to this condition with the majority of our clients that chronic aloneness is associated with depression, boredom , self-doubt, aliena‑ t i on, sleep disruption , negativity, withdrawal, and low self‑ esteem. These are certainly not the qualities that enhance the t herapist's effectiveness in clinical work ; rather, they are sure to result in the opposite —failure.

Guy (1 9 8 7) discusses the impact of isolation on the ther‑ apist. Busy clinical practices require that clients be seen in rapid succession, often precluding opportunities for contact with col‑ leagues, peers, or even family. For the most part therapists find t hemselves from first light to last, within the confines of an of‑ fice, interacting intensely with persons in distress. Emotions must be held in restraint and a stance of acceptance must pre ‑ vail. Uninterrupted by excerpts of everyday reality —a weather report, a newscast, a nonprofessional conversation —our day un ‑ folds in a limited form of existence. Crossing our threshold may be clients who cling and those that attack, those that demand and others who resist, and always those we care about who bid us good-bye. These departures can end in joy, with the launch ‑ ing of an independent being, or in tragedy with the abrupt ter‑ mination of life itself.

Of all the stresses of therapeutic practice, none is more isolating than a client ending his life. This final gesture of defeat involves not only the client but those left behind who must sort out the pieces. It is, of course, the family who is most affected by the death; it is they who must resolve their guilt, responsibil‑ ity, relief, or grief. But it is also the therapist who becomes pro ‑ foundly disturbed and isolated in the aftermath . The client's ultimate failure often becomes the greatest failure of the ther‑ apist. If only you had seen it coming, taken better precautions, or been more skilled, perhaps the person would still be alive to ‑ day. The initial reaction, of course, is not to consider our culpa‑ bility but to cut off our feelings——all the feelings—of loss, sad‑ ness, fear, guilt, inadequacy, frustration , anger.

Hobson (1985, p. 271), writing in a chapter entitled "The Heart of Darkness," mourns the loss of a client who ended her life. He tried, unsuccessfully, to cut himself off from his utter aloneness and abandonment after her suicide just as he had resisted entering her loneliness when she was alive. Yet his salvation came after he let himself feel: "As psychiatrists and analysts, and as friends, husbands, wives, and parents, we do everything possible to avoid being confronted by the terrifying depths of loneliness. In going on learning to become psycho‐ t herapists we learn skills, we practice our scales, we study psychodynamics; but we need to advance a little (and, at best, it is only a little) towards self-awareness. That means remaining in t ouch with our own cut-offness but, more important, the threat of no-being."

As we remain fixed in our efforts to give, and deaden ourselves to our need to receive, we often withdraw into numbness. This one-way intimacy —in which we are not permitted reciprocal love—leads to an interpersonal impoverishment that becomes further compounded when we isolate ourselves outside of sessions. How easily we fall prey to a distorted sense of reality! At its worst, isolation fuels a skewed sense of self and a distorted view of our client's progress. Unchecked by information others could offer, unfulfilled from the lack of healthy human contact, we insulate ourselves from all the agents that promote growth.

Yet, as dangerous as isolation can be for a therapist's growth, development, and competence , an opposite strategy is also employed by those who hide from failure in the company of others. They fear solitude and the introspection it brings. Rather than insulating themselves from unwanted information t he outside world might bring, these therapists remain detached from themselves with the assistance of others seeking also to avoid self-confrontation. An alliance is formed that perpetuates an air of activity and preoccupation . Often under the guise of professional involvement and scholarly pursuit, reflective time conveniently disappears.

At either extreme, isolation is deadly. Yet it presents a paradox in a therapist's life, for like all defenses and self-defeating behavior, a strategy of aloneness does have its benefits in combating failure. A certain amount of solitude is desirable, even necessary, for the healthy survival of the therapist. But like most behavior, when it reaches extreme proportions, not only do therapists suffer but so do their clients.

Addiction . Constantly confronted by their clients' pain and anx -
iety, feeling an urgency to help and to heal, and desperately batt ling the fears that they might not succeed, many therapists t urn to addictive agents to dull such intense feelings. Striving for success while fervently avoiding failure promotes denial, an i nherent characteristic of the addictive personality. By denying t hat impairment exists and resisting all efforts of assistance, these clinicians perpetuate the pretense. Myths of perfection, omnipotence, and control contribute to a distorted self-image. Acknowledging problems and seeking help is for clients; some t herapists hold onto a belief that if a problem were to exist, t hey could, most certainly, deal with it themselves. Colleagues unwittingly contribute to the deception by not confronting ob - viously detrimental behavior.

Consider the American Psychological Association 's faltering attempt to address the issue of their impaired colleagues. Addictive behavior is a central focus of their concern. Since 1980, when a resolution was introduced and a steering committ ee was formed, programming has been met with strong resistance. In an attempt to disseminate information and cast a spotlight on this neglected topic, in 1986 the APA published **Professionals in Distress** (Kilburg, Nathan , and Thoreson, 1986). Yet there is a general reluctance to initiate plans. Only a few states have set up programs to aid impaired psychologists and only recently has anything been done to coordinate these efforts on a national level (Denton , 1987). Undermining the progress of such critical planning is the long-held illusion that psycho - gists, as practiced healers, can heal themselves. So therapists become skillful at constructing a buffer between themselves and t he harsh realities of clinical work.

Escape through alcohol and drugs can promote the illusion of perfection and slam the door on self-scrutiny and pro - fessional improvement. Certainly each of us, in our professional lives, has encountered a colleague whose work has been impaired by alcoholism or drug addiction. Ultimately, greater losses are suffered through alcohol or drugs than by confronting one 's l i mitations or failures with clients. Loss of respect, loss of rela-t i onships, even loss of one 's license to practice may result.

Rita is a brilliant clinician. When asked about most sub-j ects in her field, she can provide you with a comprehensive discussion of the topic in question. You cannot help but be impressed by the wealth of information she has at her fingertips. In fact, it seems as if you are sitting at the feet of a wise men -tor, so fluidly do the answers come forth. But from the shadows arises a slight suspicion. Rita 's appearance seems disheveled from time to time —hair uncombed , clothes wrinkled, makeup placed haphazardly on her face. Her speech is sometimes a bit t oo rapid, the words perhaps a little slurred. She arrives late for staff meetings, and clients in the lobby mention they have been waiting for her thirty maybe forty-five minutes. And yet no one complains or seems to notice. Colleagues and interns awed by her knowledge seem to tolerate the erratic and unconventional behavior. Clients, feeling quite grateful when they are with her, only note in passing that she is often late for their appoint-ments. Students, having learned so much when she is there, shrug and nod to one another as they patiently wait.

Soon, however, this unpredictable behavior worsens. Meetings are missed, clients are not seen, classes sit there with -out an instructor. Suddenly people begin to recognize that Rita is an alcoholic. When the light snaps on, it illuminates the de-structive nature of what has occurred: Clients are mistreated, students are abandoned to sift uncertainly through new mate -rial, and trainees are left to practice new techniques without guidance on unsuspecting clients.

No one is willing to acknowledge Rita 's deteriorating be -havior. Indeed, the first revelations occur in whispers. But as the problem becomes too blatant to ignore, the ramifications ex -t end to all her professional commitments and action is taken. She is asked to leave the faculty of the university where her ini-tial contributions had been so well received. The director of the clinic where she works prohibits her from practicing there. But t he damage continues. Since Rita still has a large caseload of clients (for they are exceptionally loyal), she is still of value to other clinics—they quickly hire her and calculate the added income in their pockets.

The collusion among professionals to pretend that their colleague is healthy perpetuates harmful behavior—behavior t hat in any other circumstance would be inexcusable. Indeed, professionals are alarmingly capable of numbing themselves to obvious signals that something is wrong.

Another Kind o f Addiction . John works long hours. Seeing   clients every forty-five minutes, he accommodates both early morning and late evening requests. It is not unusual for him to leave his office at ten or eleven o 'clock at night. He has con - vinced himself he needs to work this way in order to maintain a full practice. With the exception of a professional conference, he has not taken a vacation in years. He does not wish to leave needy clients or miss a professional engagement. In fact, he involves himself in all sorts of professional activities—teach - ing, conducting seminars and workshops, serving on commit- tees. Rarely can he be overheard to say no to a professional request, and just as rarely would he set aside time for solitude, self-reflection, or nonprofessional endeavors. He proudly de - scribes himself as "too busy " and continues to heap work on himself. In this composite picture of an overcommitted ther- apist striving doggedly for recognition and success, there are as- pects of each of us. Although self-absorption in work can be marvelously invigorating—both in the joy of helping others im - prove their lives and in the satisfaction of feeling productive — this energetic spirit can be taken to excess.

Hobson (1985 , pp. 270 - 2 7 1) , speaking of the coping methods therapists use to avoid failure and confrontation with t heir driven inner nature, comments: " Using the word in a broad sense, most of us are 'addicts' in one way or another. We are devoted to compulsive actions which are ultimately dam - aging to our integrity as persons—to food ; to tranquilizers and sleeping pills; to the images on a television screen; to erudite scholarship; to committee activities; to dependence on friends,

spouses, or analysts; to recording our dreams; and to 'religions'
such as 'Christianity ' or golf. And we get 'withdrawal symp -
t oms ' when we cannot pursue those activities by means of
which we deny the terror of non-existence, the void of no -
being ." Constant activity and professional engagements keep
our pace at high speed so that exhaustion replaces the opportu -
nity to process the day 's events. The next day brings m ore -
more clients, more phone calls, more meetings, more activity.

We think we have become experts at self-deception, yet
reality intrudes from time to time to shake our composure.
Sometimes the voice of truth becomes loud enough to drown
out the myths we so stubbornly uphold. Rita, after being hospitalized numerous times, is painstakingly attempting to recon -
struct her professional life; John , however, does not yet see the
negative pattern he is creating and the destructive nature of his
workaholic life-style.

Conceding Failure. But the challenges of failure can also be side-

stepped, surprisingly, by **admitting** one 's mistakes and misjudgments and saying "I have failed." In this variation of self-decep-
ti on, confessions are made but finalized with statements such as
"it was above my head ," " I didn 't know what to do , " or "yes, I
used poor judgment." Then the discussion is quickly terminated. Taking full responsibility for a failure by giving lip-service
t o it can sometimes prevent the possibility of self-discovery as
effectively as the attempt at full denial. In each case, further
self-examination is aborted and the threat of risk escaped. Con -
ceding defeat does not prepare a team for their next game, a
candidate for the next election, a scientist for the next experiment. It does put off the critics, though, and deflect emotion .
It gets the accused off the hook and allows them to slide away
from responsibility and don the cloak of safety.

There are, perhaps, as many ways to avoid failure as there
are practitioners. And, for the most part, these attempts only
perpetuate a m yth —of omnipotence, success, perfection. They
keep us in the dark, in a place of our own choosing, where we
can feel safe and secure and filter out any information that
might challenge our precious self-portrait. Despite attempts to

hide from the ominous cloud of failure, however, all these maneuvers are in vain. We cannot avoid it, no matter what we try,
for in our self-deception we are certain, eventually, to fail. Sup-
pressing all the evidence does not make it disappear. It simply
makes it more powerful and makes us more dedicated to its
extinction.

Liberating ourselves from this battle will allow us to view
failure not as an enemy to be destroyed , but as an ally to be
consulted. We will no longer need to expend so much effort en -
gaged in a battle that is not worth fighting, a battle that, in any
case, we will ultimately and painfully lose.

4

Benefits of
Confronting Imperfection

It is the nature of failure to provide the grist for learning, reflection, reconsideration, for change, risk, and imagination. New ideas arise not from repetition but from risk, from new int egrations, from altering factors and variables to accommodate new changes. The human being has almost unlimited potential for creativity, for discovering better, more profound , more useful ways of living, for strengthening the self, for rebounding from defeat.

Within the process of therapy itself, Hammer (1972 , p. 14) points out that "regression always precedes real progression and growth ." When things proceed most haltingly is when "the patient first takes a backward step so to speak, by permitting himself to enter into full communion with those repressed and painful aspects of his rejected self which then permits the forward advance—in terms of a greater sense of integrative wholeness, liberation or growth —to really take place."

The Uses of Defeat

The history of the human race is a documentary of failure. Every significant advance in our culture and technology has been won by repeated trial and error. Every great writer, artist, architect, politician, athlete, and scientist has experienced de feat many times in life. It was failure that motivated almost a t hird of the U.S. presidents to seek the office that had been denied them earlier. Defeat only made Jefferson , Jackson , Adams, Roosevelt, and others more determined to win the next time. It was Van Gogh 's complete rejection by critics that led him to languish in isolated despair, but also to create such original and passionate work. It was critical scorn by peers, imprisonment, and exile that led writers such as Dostoyevsky and Solzhenitsyn t o create singularly stirring portraits of alienation and angst.

Experiences are neither positive nor negative. They challenge us simply to be open to learning, to consider new ideas, to take in information and filter it through our own perceptions. Lessons afford us a chance to risk, to change, to grow, to be creative, to remain vitally connected to the present. They allow us t o be flexible yet grounded in our own base of knowledge. They do not demand doing something the "right" way or require us t o find "the answer." We take in information , sift and sort, distill , in te grate, synthesize, implement, practice, and constantly reassess. We engage in the process without overemphasizing the product.

A study of failure can encourage us to accept it as a part of life just as we must accept the inevitability of death. Even death, the ultimate failure, evolved as a better idea among creatures whose body cells had become too specialized to con- t i nue the immortality guaranteed by perpetual mitosis. In the words of a thoughtful biologist: "Thus did death become a handy tool of change and evolution. For all the multi-celled structures that neglected to adopt it became extinct" (Murchie, 1978, p. 526). Some sociobiologists view even suicide, the ultimate failure of will, as serving a useful social function by removing mentally unstable individuals from the world. Repro - ductive fitness of kin is thereby enhanced by eliminating a po - tential gene pool that may be tainted (Wenegrat, 1984). Indeed, a frequent fantasy of those who attempt self-destruction is the feeling of being a burden to others.

These examples, reframing death in functional terms, t ake the benefits of organic failure to an extreme. Nevertheless, as we often point out to clients, it is usually one 's interpretation of an incident that creates its meaning. We therefore invite you t o view this exploration of failure as helpful rather than threat- ening. We do so not to rationalize our mistakes and make our lives a little easier. Nor do we advocate complete acceptance of our misjudgments as simple extensions of our humanity. None of us would ever choose failure over success any more than Van Gogh would have chosen ostracism over acclaim. Rather the point is this: By studying failure, reframing its negative context, using it to learn and grow, we can become more effective in the future.

How Failure Helps the Therapist

Failure is a signal that something is not working the way it was intended. It is part of a feedback loop that provides information on the impact of our actions. This information , if acknowledged, allows us to adjust our behavior so that negative results are not likely to be repeated. In therapy situations Haley (1980), Madanes (198 1), and Fisch, Weakland, and Segal (1 9 8 2) point out that therapists who operate strategically need not ever know which interventions will work in effecting client changes as long as they pay attention to what does not work or has not worked before. A prime example of a therapeutic approach that values failure as much as success is one in which the clinician does not expect or need to be right during initial helping efforts. A respect for process, a belief in the client's resources, faith that healing results from struggle and experimentation , allows a therapeutic stance of patience and tolerance for failure.

A mother and father were on the verge of divorce because of mutual frustration in trying to control an unruly teenager. After having already consulted a half-dozen well-meaning mental health professionals from every discipline, their morale was depleted; they felt angry, confused, and helpless. Recently they had placed their faith, hesitantly, in the hands of a clinician who was a great respecter of failure. She spent the first several sessions simply cataloging all the dozens of parenting interventi ons, discipline strategies, and expert advice that had already been tried and failed. She even tried a few suggestions of her own.

This particular child, however, was a master of counter-t errorist activities and always discovered a way to circumvent t he best-laid plans. Limit setting, family communication , reinforcement schedules, even paradoxical maneuvers in which the

child was given complete freedom to do as she liked—all met
with disaster. Since this therapist gave herself permission to fail
and had warned the parents not to expect too much too quickly,
she believed she had plenty of opportunities to experiment.
When she counseled the couple to console one another, to work
on their marriage instead of their belligerent child, the girl was
promptly expelled for another school infraction. By this time
t he therapist had compiled quite a long list of therapeutic op -
t i ons that had failed—including everything from family therapy
and Ritalin to l ough Love support groups. Although the therapist still had no clear idea what might make a difference, she
felt quite confident about a lot of things that would not work,
so she felt no need to repeat them . Eventually, through con -
t i nued trial and error, she discovered a combination of solutions
t hat proved effective. (By that time, of course, the teenager
may have felt sorry for all the professionals she had stumped
and gave up the resistance out of boredom .) In this example of
clients and therapist coping with failure, it becomes evident that
struggle is expected and met not with frustration but with an
attitude of acceptance and further experimentation .

   When failure is treated with as much respect as success, it
becomes a valuable source of information about the world and
t he forces that interact within it. Each shot that falls wide of
t he target can be noted as useful information that will be helpful
in the next attempt. And if the archer is calm in spirit, free of
self-critical judgments and pressure to perform according to
some prescribed standard, she or he may simply shoot, observe
t he results, and then shoot again with more accuracy.

The Value of Persistence

   Failure is helpful to therapists in ways other than providing information about the impact of behavior. In fact, our
whole culture has been shaped by philosophies that emerged
from initial failure. It was the persistence of Aristotle, Bacon,
Galileo, Descartes, Newton, and Locke reacting against the prevalent view that led to the discovery of nature as we know it
(Hayward, 1984). This is most certainly true in our own field,

t oo, in which Freud encountered so much resistance and struggled throughout his life to be accepted as a legitimate scientist. Feelings of isolation and rejection only further encouraged him t o follow his personal vision unencumbered by the traditional neurology of his time.

The same could be said for one of Freud 's contempo raries. As a young man, Albert Einstein consistently failed to win any academic appointment that would have provided collegial contact, extensive library and research facilities, as well as financial support. Instead, Einstein worked for seven years as a minor civil servant in the Swiss patent office. Yet his tedious j ob reading patent applications afforded him the opportunity to t hink in isolation, to hone his understanding of technical specifications, and to express himself concisely. Although an exiled scholar and failed academic, Einstein was able to develop his mind far beyond that of a successful professional clone. In the words of a biographer, Einstein 's "isolation accounts for his broad view of specific scientific problems—he ignored the de ‑ t ailed arguments of others because he was unaware of them . It also shows a courage beyond the call of scientific duty , submis‑ sion to the inner compulsion which was to drive him on through ‑ out life and for which he was willing to sacrifice everything " (Clark, 1971, p. 86).

While we are certainly not advocating that therapists isolate themselves, ignore conventional thinking and current research, and embrace a life-style filled with rejection, we are pointing out ways in which distinguished thinkers have used failure to their advantage. Some of our field 's most prominent leaders have been fiercely independent truth seekers throughout t heir lives—open to constructive comments from their clients and colleagues but impervious to outright rejection. Neither Freud nor Adler, Skinner nor Rogers, Wolpe nor Frankl, Ellis nor Haley, had an easy time getting their ideas examined. They were ignored, ridiculed, criticized, hounded , and only reluctantly accepted. Yet the initial failures of creative therapists only strengthened their resolve. In the case of Carl Jung, for exam ‑ ple, expelled from the Viennese Psychoanalytic Society and summarily dismissed by his mentor Freud as a heretic, his fail‑

ure became a turning point in his own evolution: "After the
break with Freud, all my friends and acquaintances dropped
away. My book was declared to be rubbish; I was a mystic; and
t hat settled the matter. . But I had foreseen my isolation and
harbored no illusion about the reactions of my so-called friends.
That was a point I had considered beforehand . I had known t
hat everything was at stake, and that I had to take a stand for my
convictions" (Jung , 1961, pp. 167-168).

Taking a stand for one 's convictions—and living with the
consequences—is one of the values we hope to impart to our clients. From the knowledge that it is impossible to win the ap -
proval of everyone all of the time, to help every client, to succeed at every challenge, emerges a preparation for failure and a
respect for its inherent value. Failure can help the therapist, just
as it helps the client, to mobilize greater commitment and energy
t oward one 's goals.

Failure as a Stimulus

It seems ironic that so many therapists were raised in dysfunctional families. The children of alcoholics, abusive parents,
broken homes, grew from their amateur standing as family res-
cuers into professional helpers. Many of us found our way into
t he field while recuperating from our own failures. In the pro -
cess of overcoming feelings of inadequacy while in training pro -
grams, or working on personal issues in our own therapy, many
clinicians learned to help others overcome their failures by first
conquering their own. This phenomenon is not unique just to
our field. Of the three hundred or so most eminent people of
t he past century, four out of ten had fathers who were failures.
Goertzel, Goertzel, and Goertzel (1978), in their study of famous personalities, discovered that fathers who were imagina-
tive and driving, yet failure prone, encouraged in their children a
striving for innovation, creativity, and persistence to succeed.
From the failure of one generation springs the spectacular success of their offspring.

If John Shakespeare had not resigned in disgrace as his
t own 's mayor, William would never have fled to London deter-

mined to redeem his family name. It was Carl Jung 's contempt for his sickly, bankrupt, depressed father which fueled his ambi- t i on to gain fame and fortune. Failure-prone fathers can become models for their successful offspring by taking risks, experi- menting with the unknown , and insulating themselves from crit- icism. Yet these children were able to learn from their fathers' mistakes and give that extra push to succeed. Because they were accustomed to disappointment, they were able to develop self- reliance. They learned to live with instability and uncertainty in life because of their fathers' precarious earning power. They evolved a need to be useful, to chip in and help the family. This was certainly Charles Dickens's response when his father was t hrown in debtors prison, Tolstoy 's reaction to the gambling debts his father incurred, and Einstein 's productive urges in re- action to a father who could never stay employed .

It is not that the majority of therapists have had a failure- prone parent or even come from a dysfunctional family. The point is that even these troubled environments did not preclude its members from flourishing. Early conflict, family tension, and exposure to failure need not destroy a person 's character; on the contrary, it often encourages children to become more resourceful adults.

Time Out for Introspection

One consequence of failure is that it stops people dead in t heir tracks. Out of necessity, one has to pause and consider what went wrong and why. The aftermath of failure is a period of reflection, reassessment; it is a time to regroup, to question oneself, and to plan new directions.

Consider the impact of failure on the U.S. space program . Prior to the Challenger explosion on national television, NASA struggled to maintain its overburdened schedule of twenty -four space shots per year on a shoestring budget that frazzled every- one 's nerves. Since the inquiry into the incident, uncovering widespread incompetence and mismanagement, things have changed considerably. In the words of one expert: "Sometimes nothing succeeds like failure.   . There followed a few ritual resignations, and now NASA has its reward. It hasn 't launched a shuttle for nineteen months and won 't have to for another year or more; at peak, the shuttle schedule has been cut in half. No – body will complain if a launch is delayed again. And the agency has 35 percent more money in its pocket" (Martz, 1987, p. 34).

It seems to take an occasional disaster to get our atten – t i on. There is nothing like an angry client to force us to con– sider whether our behavior might be provocative. There is noth – ing like the threat of a lawsuit to motivate us to keep better records. There is nothing like an attempted suicide to get us to question our sensitivity and diagnostic skills. There is nothing like a client ending treatment prematurely to encourage greater flexibility. In many cases we experience, initially, a profound period of doubt that gradually gives way to a determination to piece things together. The result of this inner journey is a more aware and enlightened human being. Questioning professionals become wiser, more skilled, more accepting of mistakes in themselves and others.

A physician orders four separate urine tests for a patient who has been showing signs of pregnancy for weeks. Although t he woman claims that she feels pregnant, all test results are negative. The doctor, therefore, performs an abortion to clear out the dead fetus, only to discover that the baby was alive. He confesses his mistake in anguish to his patient and later reflects on his responsibility and his humanity : "Mistakes are an inevi– t able part of everyone's life. They happen-, they hurt —ourselves and others. They demonstrate our fallibility. Shown our mis– t akes and forgiven them , we can grow, perhaps in some small way become better people. Mistakes, understood this way, are a process, a way we connect with one another and our deepest self" (Hilfiker, 1984, p. 60).

Appreciation for Serendipity

A respect for failure teaches the therapist that accidental happenings can mean as much as that which is intentional. This is not only true for the incidental benefits of learning that was spontaneous or unintended , but for the serendipitous nature of t he universe as well. An open mind free of judgment, criticism, and preconceptions, a mind that refuses to fix labels of success or failure, allows one to discover the unknown or the invisible.

Such an open mind allowed inventors to convert disaster i nto major advances in science. The principle of the hot air bal‐ loon, for example, was discovered when the wife of Jacques Montgolfier ruined her petticoat by hanging it over a fire to dry. Similarly, the first X ray was taken quite by accident. Wilhelm Konrad von Roentgen spoiled his photographic film by hurriedly tossing a key on it near a cathode tube that emitted streams of electrons. When he returned from lunch, he discovered the image of the key superimposed over the botched photographs. And a final instance of significant advancement through seren‐ dipitous failure took place in a biochemical laboratory in which Alexander Fleming negligently left a germ culture uncovered overnight. His failure to conform to standard research precau‐ t i ons allowed specks of mold to fall into the dish, thereby de ‐ stroying the bacteria he had been studying. He later isolated this antibacterial mold and experimented with its effect on other germs. Had it not been for this bit of luck, combined with his lapse in procedure, penicillin might never have been discovered. Of course, twenty years of intense scientific study of microbes and an open mind made Fleming the ideal candidate to recog‐ nize his error and learn from its consequence.

In these and other instances in the laboratory or ther‐ apist's chambers, a keen sense of observation permits the practi‐ t i oner to turn defeat into dramatic success. Telling a hypochon ‐ driacal client that she should attend medical school and become her own physician, advising an overprotective mother that she should immediately remove her child from the classroom so she can be with him all the time —these maneuvers evolved from fail‐ ing at conventional reflection, interpretation , and intervention. They serendipitously grew out of the moment with a creative flash. Such comments lead to new perceptions and, ultimately, t o change. Perhaps this is how paradoxical maneuvers were dis‐ covered in which the therapist orders a client to engage in some activity that will immediately be disobeyed —thereby curing the presenting complaint. This might also explain how Freud stum ‐

bled upon the unconscious, the value of catharsis, and his no-
t i on of transference in the therapeutic relationship.

While we may never know the actual series of events that
led Peris or Rogers or Frankl or Ellis or others to deviate from
t heir psychoanalytic training (as they themselves may not even
have known), we might well imagine that chance and failure
played significant parts. If Victor Frankl had not been in a concentration camp, had not in horror watched his family and
friends perish, had not had his previous beliefs about human na-
t ure fail him, he may never have formulated the nucleus of logo-
therapy. The same could be said for Ellis's ineffectual experiences as an analyst, his need to be more engaging and active in
sessions, and many random events that coalesced in the embodi-
ment of a cognitive-based therapy that reflected his personal
way of being.

The therapist on the lookout for the unexpected is likely t o
view negative outcomes as opportunities for further study of
mysterious phenomena. Failure draws one 's attention to a result in
need of explanation ; it is a call to creativity and further experimentation.

Learning One 's Limits

Performance in any endeavor is improved through up-
grading one 's weaknesses. Kramer (1987, p. 18) reviews the
values of error specifically in psychiatric practice:

> Therapists' errors are essential to empathic diagno-
> sis. When we are aroused by the hysteric —instead —
> we take on a posture toward the patient which is
> ordinarily unacceptable in the physician. Likewise,
> when we are depressed by the depressive. These
> mistakes, when recognized, lead to the treatment
> plan.
>   Counter-transference in the narrow sense—
> t hose perceptions in the therapist elicited by the
> t r ansference —is error. We intend to see the patient
> without distortion , but repeatedly we fail. Instead,

our vision is clouded by the patient's expectations— j udged by ordinary standards, we truly misapprehend —and our catching ourselves in this error is the basis for much of our work.

Whenever we run up against a brick wall, rather than regarding our frustration as failure, we might instead conclude t hat our view of the world is too constricted, our theory not comprehensive enough. When quantum physics was discovered, it did not replace Newtonian physics but included it despite its li mitations. "To say that we have made a major new discovery about nature is one side of a coin. The other side of the coin is t o say that we have found the limits of our previous theories" (Zukav, 1979, p. 19). This, of course, is hardly a distressing event; on the contrary, it is a joyous occasion. We should celebrate when we find the exception to the rule or discover that a proven technique fails to produce the predicted response. We expand our knowledge, develop our theories, improve our performance with every negative result. Albert Einstein looked at t he discovery of limitations as a way to improve his ideas. In his view, "creating a new theory is not like destroying an old barn and erecting a skyscraper in its place. It is rather like climbing a mountain , gaining new and wider views, discovering unexpected connections between our starting point and its rich environment. But the point from which we started out still exists and can be seen, although it appears smaller and forms a tiny part of our broad view gained by the mastery of the obstacles on our adventurous way up" (Einstein and Infeld, 1938, p. 31).

The field of psychiatry and psychopharmacology is replete with instances in which an investigator was searching for one compound , was frustrated in the effort, and ended up discovering clinical applications in other directions. Chlorpromazine, an antipsychotic medication, was discovered not by a psychiatrist but by the surgeon Laborit, who was looking for an agent that would control shock. By seeking to inhibit the auton - omous nervous system in order to reduce surgical stress, he found that the calming effects might be even more helpful in t r eating agitation among psychiatric patients. In a similar case,

Roland Kuhn was hired to study the effects of Imipramine on schizophrenics but found the results to be discouraging. He did, however, observe that this dead end led him to experiment with t he drug 's antidepressant properties.

Similarly, the therapist learns about the limits of her or his capacity for understanding through results that initially seem less than promising. It is only after rethinking our hypoth – esis and reformulating new premises that we may construct more comprehensive and useful theories. A similar scenario oc – curs every time we return from a workshop that presents some new therapeutic approach. We often find that whereas the in – structor was quite elegant in applying a particular strategy, when we attempt to duplicate the effort exactly the result falls short. Workshop participants often find that back in the office t hey cannot quite master the interventions that Virginia Satir, Jay Haley, or Richard Bandler demonstrated on stage. It is only after trying the prescribed regimen again and again that we be – gin to make the necessary adjustments that account for differ – ences in our own personality, therapeutic style, and clientele. With each unsuccessful attempt to apply some new interven – ti on, we gain greater wisdom about our own limitations, yet, in t he process, uncover new possibilities.

Risk and Failure

In his treatise on risk taking, Keyes (1985) collected a few quotes pertinent to the subject of failure implicit in being venturesome. Sports psychologist Bruce Ogilvie: "The great athletes that I have interviewed do not dwell upon their losses but concentrate upon that part of their performance that lim – it ed their excellence." Aspiring comedian Lorretta Colla on how failure helps her gain strength: " I mean, once you 've told me to 'get da fuck offa da stage,' what more can you say to me ? " And Woody Allen, obsessed with failure in his films, offers: " Failure is a sure sign that you 're not playing it safe, that you are still ex – perimenting, still taking creative risks. . . . If y o u 're succeeding t oo much, you 're doing something wrong ."

Failure, then, becomes nothing more or less than a special

form of encouragement—either to follow one 's convictions or to change direction altogether. In either case, it is apparent that all decisive actions involve the risks of the unknown . In therapy, venturing any response involves the possibility of denial, regression, hostility, or rejection by the client. And the more dramatic t he intervention, the greater the potential may be for rapid im provement.

Therapists who are conservative in their approach may, t herefore, see steady, gradual progress. Treatment will probably be lengthy, predictable, and controlled —especially desirable circumstances for clients who have a tendency toward impulsivity or who are operating at the edge of control. Such treatments may fail when the therapist has neglected to follow the prescribed regimen or when the client becomes impatient for results.

At the other end of the continuum , therapists who apply provocative or intrusive techniques may facilitate a client's changes more quickly. Practitioners who rely on brief, strategic approaches, who employ confrontation , behavioral techniques, hypnosis, or other interventions that treat symptoms in a direct fashion, can be beneficial or harmful in a much more dramatic way than their traditional colleagues. The potential for failure, t herefore, has a proportional relationship to the risks of treatment. Most therapists try to balance these two factors at a level t hat seems personally appropriate. Whereas one professional could never imagine using bioenergetic therapy because of fears of releasing unbridled emotions or reluctance to follow relati vely untested procedures, another would find it completely unacceptable to rely on a conventional "talking cure " that seems t oo primitive and slow.

It is not that we divide ourselves into two camps—the reckless and the inflexible—but rather that each of us chooses an acceptable level of risk in our practice. Depending on our ability to recover from disappointment, our vulnerability to attack, our experience in defending ourselves, our values related t o risk, our whole way of being, we may operate anywhere from t he most reactionary position to the edge of respectability.

The fear of failure helps the therapist to proceed cauti ously in order to protect the client from ill-conceived interventions. Yet the fear of taking calculated risks may also prevent the therapist from acting in the client's best interest. This could involve attempting a role play even when the practitioner must overcome her or his own inhibitions. It may mean that the therapist must conquer internal apprehensions and insecurities to challenge a client's thinking or a colleague's misguided assessment. failure results when the risks exceed the potential gain; this correlation keeps us in line, exploring the unknowns, but within safe parameters.

Pretending to Fail

The legendary frontiersman Daniel Boone once simulated failure in order to dupe his enemies. Eventually charged with a dozen counts of treason for his actions, Boone risked hanging as a consequence. In an account of his court martial, the historian Allen Eckert (1973) relates how during the Revolutionary War Captain Boone surrendered himself and his men to the Shawnee Indians and their British allies without a fight. Furthermore , Boone readily admitted he led the enemy to his own camp, negotiated its surrender, agreed to become adopted by Chief Black Fish as his son, and voluntarily traveled to the British stronghold where he conspired with the generals to defeat American forces. During his trial Boone made little effort to defend himself, refused counsel to represent him, and listened t o his community in Boonesborough scream for his conviction and death. His friends and foes alike were unanimously con - vinced of his guilt, and as the evidence and testimony mounted , it s eemed certain he would die.

It was only at the end of his trial, when Boone took the stand to tell his side of the story, that we learn he had con - structed an elaborate scheme to trick his enemies. Knowing an attack was imminent against his half-built forces, Boone dis- t r acted the enemy from his main stronghold by volunteering his own patrol's capture. He joined the Indians only to learn of t heir plans and sabotage their weapons. He went to Fort Detroit t o plant misinformation so the British would underestimate t heir task in conquering Boonesborough. Because of this decep -

t i on in which Boone pretended to betray his friends and coun ⎯ try, he was able to stall the attack for many months. And when Boonesborough did come under siege, the inhabitants were more than ready to repel the invasion. The Indian rifles had all misfired. The British had been persuaded to leave their artillery behind. And because they expected a quick surrender as Boone had promised, they were not prepared for a major fight. Thus what appeared to be a tragic failure on the part of a single indi⎯ vidual aided the survival of a whole community .

The pretense of failure can also play a part in successful therapy. There are times when, for the sake of allowing a client t o save face or win an argument, some therapists will back down and deliberately fail. In many paradoxical interventions, for ex ⎯ ample, the therapist predicts what will not occur or requests the client to do something that is designed to be disobeyed. And t here are times when, for the sake of a client's good, a therapist will follow Boone 's strategy of acknowledging defeat. This ma⎯ neuver is most commonly used when parental support must be won in order to help a child.

In one such case a father was particularly critical of his son 's therapist. Whenever the adolescent spoke of his therapist's wisdom or kindness, the father became enraged and eventually pulled him out of treatment because of his jealous and threat⎯ ened feelings. Wanting very badly to help the child, the ther⎯ apist swallowed his pride and telephoned the father. He apolo ⎯ gized for mishandling the case, readily acknowledged a number of mistakes the father pointed out, let him blow off steam and criticize his treatment. To every accusation the father offered, t he therapist agreed and asked for assistance and advice. Even⎯ tually, the father asked to come in and further straighten out t he therapist's thinking which, naturally, led to a more sup⎯ portive alliance. The father saved face in the eyes of his son; the boy was able to continue working with the therapist with the father's now enthusiastic support; and the therapist learned a l ot about the value of failure. Once he allowed himself to relin⎯ quish his control and no longer needed to win every confronta ⎯ t i on with the father, his loss became everyone else's gain.

Presenting a Human Model

In this chapter we have borrowed many examples from history to illustrate the benefits of failure in promoting advancement in science, culture, and quality of life. We have attempted to cast failure in a positive light as a potential source in furthering growth of the therapist, the client, and the treatment process. In recalling that Freud first became famous by advocating cocaine as a magic potion for well-being, or that Henry Ford designed a car constructed entirely from soybeans and never sold a single model, we can perhaps forgive ourselves for our own shortcomings.

Misalliances commonly occur between client and therapist. The goal, according to Langs (1978), is for therapists to recognize their mistakes and explore them with the client. Such analysis "must take precedence over all other therapeutic work, since it is essential to the restoration of a proper therapeutic alliance" (p. 153). It is as much the person of the therapist as the methodologies employed that inspires clients to change. These modeling effects are often more useful when the therapist is viewed not only as powerful, nurturing, and competent but also as a human being with imperfections and struggles of his own. Jourard, in his seminal studies on therapists' self-disclosure, evidences its benefit to the therapeutic process in encouraging clients to be more open and free in revealing the shadows and struggles of their lives. Of interest here is the success of Alcoholics Anonymous and the effectiveness of therapy when conducted by a counselor who is a recovering alcoholic.

Self-disclosure is commonly used by therapists to demonstrate ways in which they have experienced problems similar to the client's. This technique, for example, may involve a personal confession of failure to a client: "You're feeling discouraged because your learning disabilities prevent you from succeeding in college. It is tough you can't read well or understand numbers. You're right, it's not fair that you should be stuck with these handicaps, doomed to fail in academic subjects. But you are not the only one in the world who has weaknesses. I barely gradu-

ated from high school and only got into college on probation .
To this day, I feel intimidated by math and science although I
wanted so badly to graduate that I got extra help and learned
t r icks for avoiding subjects I couldn 't handle. I forgave myself
for being flawed and, yes, even stupid in some areas. And just
because you feel like a failure in school doesn 't mean you
can 't succeed in other areas of life. We are alike in that we both
have our limitations; but they can be overcome if you will be
patient with yourself, yet persistent in going after what you
want."

Presenting a model of humanness to clients is done not
only through self-disclosure of past failures that have been con –
quered, but also with interactions in the present. The technique
of "immediacy " is often used when the therapist discusses feelings or events that are occurring at the moment in order to focus
attention on a specific behavior requiring comment. In addi-
t i on to describing the client's behavior as it is occurring, immediacy interventions can be used to accentuate the fallibility of
t he therapist's behavior. Far from being a perfect specimen who
never makes mistakes, the therapist occasionally misjudges a
situation or offers an inappropriate statement. When this hap –
pens, it is essential for the therapist to acknowledge the error:

- "Maybe I wasn 't listening fully. Let's go over that again."
- "I was making assumptions about you that were biased by
  my own experience."
- "I really was way off target that time, wasn 't I?"

Further, it requires courage and humility for a therapist to say
"I don 't know " in response to a client's plea for answers.

Admitting mistakes, errors, and misjudgments can some-
t i mes initiate a turning point during treatment. Suddenly the
t herapist is viewed not only as an expert but as a human being
who, except for training, motivation , and hard work, is very
much like the client. This recognition makes a significant impact not only in sessions, but in our lives as well. Failure is a
reminder of our fallibility; it thus fosters a sense of modesty

and counteracts the tendency toward narcissism that is so prevalent in our profession. The therapist who occasionally fails, who accepts these lapses as indicative of an imperfect being who is t r ying very hard to grow, will maintain feelings of competence and yet become a model of self-acceptance.

5

Basic Lapses
and Mistakes
of Beginners

Failure is useful in the sense that it improves future performance. We contend that a therapist's growth is not only facilitated by demonstrating what works, but by recognizing what does not work. The lapses in judgment, the miscalculations in timing and pace, the misapplications of techniques or interventions that are made by beginning therapists are particularly instructive because they represent fundamental errors. What the novice does wrong reminds the more experienced therapist about the dangers of ignoring the value of basic therapeutic strategies.

What the Novice Can Teach Us

Reading a transcript or listening to an interview of a therapist's first sessions provides an illuminating experience, as professors and supervisors know well. We might hear such obvious lapses as a barrage of close-ended questions or nervous chattering to avoid any form of silence. While the veteran would rarely commit such transgressions, we cannot help but notice how we may occasionally make similar errors in diluted form . It is for t his very reason that experienced therapists volunteer their time beyond the call of duty to work in supervisory roles—not only from a sense of commitment to educate those who are just starting out, but because we can learn so much from their mistakes. Their enthusiasm becomes contagious, and their inquisitive minds, awkwardness, and blatant errors make therapy much more comprehensible.

It is a common experience for those who teach introduc - tory' courses to watch their own therapy efforts become sharper as attention is once again devoted to the fundamental skills of li stening, reflecting, simply being with the client. By monitor - ing the rambling language of students, we become more concise in our own communications. By pointing out the beginner's i mpatience in trying to force compliance in sessions, we notice ourselves backing off more easily. Thus the beginner's experience with failure provides valuable lessons for every therapist.

Zukav (1979) writes of the value in studying the beginner 's mind —especially with regard to the innocent spirit that allows one to "see the world as it is, and not as it appears according to what we know about it " (pp. 117 -1 1 8). He continues t o applaud the benefits of a simplistic sense that is often lost t hrough experience. The beginner is naive, free of habits, doubt- ful, inquiring.

Robertiello and Schoenwolf (1 9 8 7) separate the mistakes of beginners into two categories. The first—technical errors— occur in the early years of practice. They result from faulty se- l ection of techniques, misdiagnosis, failure to extract latent from manifest content, and a less than optimal attitude. The second type of error is more insidious since the therapist is not aware that anything dangerous has occurred. These unconscious transgressions involve some variety of the therapist's counter- t r ansference and counter-resistance. The authors present several examples of how the clinician's intense feelings—erotic, aggressive, defensive, competitive, contemptuous , fearful, resentful, or shameful—may land him or her in difficulty.

Jenkins, Hildebrand, and Lask (1982) mention those instances in which failure is hardly the result of the therapist's overactive imagination or unresolved fears, but stems rather from i ncompetence or misjudgment. The beginning therapist, in particular, makes a number of errors handling resistance and transference issues. In such cases the fear of failure is quite constructive in t hat it provokes healthy reluctance and caution when working with people 's lives. Van Hooseand Kottler (1 9 8 5) enumerate oth - er examples of therapists ' failures, especially those actions that inadvertently foster the client's dependency. Beginning therapists are apt to underestimate their power and influence in the therapeutic relationship.

Beginners are not the only ones who fall victim to feelings of insecurity and inadequacy. Indeed, the supervisors they so highly regard may also experience fears of failure. They may experience anxieties about doing supervision and be reluctant t o seek consultation when problems arise for fear of tarnishing t heir reputation (Jackel, 1982, pp. 16 -1 7). The same questions t hat terrify the student reverberate through the mind of the novice supervisor: "What if the student asks an obvious quest i on that I can 't begin to address? What if the trainee drops out of supervision? Will I be liked and worthy of respect? Can I con — t r i bute to this therapist's growth ? " (Alonso, 1985, p. 57).

Similar to the beginner's experiences described in this chapter, Alonso (1985 , p. 88) elucidates a host of the m entor 's needs that hamper supervision—the need to be admired, to rescue, to be in control, to compete , to be loved. A further interference in supervision, as in therapy, may be spillover from stress in the supervisor's personal or professional life. Just as the t herapist in training requires supervision in negotiating the many turns of clinical life, so too may supervisors need collegial counsel as well as personal therapy.

When asked the question "How did you know this was a failure?" the typical response of a beginner is, "My expectations were not m et ." This answer refers to expectations of where the client should be, how quickly the client should get there, and how effective the therapist should be in making this happen . Caught up in expectations for instant success and immediate competence, beginning therapists tend to have a narrow perspective of therapy. Armed with a specific set of techniques and a particular theoretical orientation , beginning therapists believe t hey are bound to succeed if only they can implement what t hey learned in graduate school.

When we study the mistakes of beginners, we are reminded of the errors we have made in our own development as therapists. We return to the territory through which we have traveled and recognize the obstacles we have confronted . In so doing, our awareness is heightened and our complacency van—

ishes. Reexperiencing our mistakes as beginners gives us an op - portunity to realize how far we have come and recapture the excitement and passion of our work.

The Struggle with Responsibility

One of the most common themes throughout the experience of beginning therapists is that of taking full responsibility for the client's "cure ." After hearing the client's initial concerns, t he therapist assumes he or she knows what is best and sets in motion a whole process of events to realize this goal. Instead of providing the opportunity for the client to take action, the therapist springs into motion . Calls are made to community resources, a list of suggested contacts is handed to the client, books on key topics are offered. The therapist not only shows clients the menu but tells them what they should eat. June , a recent graduate in clinical psychology, was employed at a com - munity mental health agency and was counseling a single young woman who was considering an abortion . Not only did June structure the dialogue so that the woman was convinced that an abortion was the best solution, but in her zeal to be helpful, she made all the arrangements for the procedure to take place the next day!

"I got him to change jobs ," "I finally persuaded her to leave her boyfriend ," " I kept her alive after her mother died " — such statements reflect the beginning therapist's sense of over- i mportance and the inherent danger of establishing a dependent relationship. Hand in hand with this concept of overzealous re- sponsibility is the trepidation new therapists feel in making an i ntervention that does not fit their training mode. One false word, they fear, can do irreparable harm . They imagine the client will disintegrate with the first inappropriate or poorly timed statement.

Helping a client succeed because of the **therapist's** needs
results in the therapist doing too much of the client's work. Trainees are told by experienced mentors that if they are work - ing harder than the client, something is wrong. Yet this message is often forgotten as new therapists continue to invite all sorts

of responsibilities—not only because they need to succeed, but also because they do not trust the clients' inherent ability to re-solve their own issues. Feeling that they should be all-knowing and all-powerful, many neophyte therapists assume responsibil- it y for the client's cure.

A Beginner's Mind

The mind of the beginning therapist—and the novice's preoccupation with responsibility for outcome —are illustrated in t he poignant words of a young woman who wished, more than anything, to be an exceptional clinician. As presented in Chap - t er Two, all six questions that plague the therapist are apparent in the following example:

> There 's a little girl that I had been seeing after her father was killed. Her mother brought her to me because she was not doing well in school. She was not very trusting at all and it took a really long t i me to get through to her. She wouldn 't let me t ouch her or play games with her. After quite some ti me we began to make contact with one another and the sessions became a lot more comfortable for both of us. Unfortunately , however, her school per-formance didn 't improve much.
>
> The child 's teacher eventually wrote me a note essentially saying what a lousy job I was doing — t he kid still couldn 't read and was a pain for others t o deal with. Both she and the mother implied it was my fault, that there was something I should be doing that I wasn 't. I'm already pretty insecure; I haven 't been doing this for very long. But that crit- icism really got to me.
>
> In the very next session I abandoned our usual routine of playing games and having a good t i me with one another. I thought it was time for me to use some more forceful interventions to get i mmediate results so the mother and teacher would

get off my back. So I tried some behavior modifi-
cation stuff that I wasn 't too familiar with but came
highly recommended from a colleague. I was just
so scared that this little girl would get pulled out of
t r eatment unless I could work some magic.

It became obvious that what I had worked
so hard to build with this child quickly fell apart
once I resorted to these techniques. I felt her draw
away from me, and lose all the trust we had built
together. I felt so sorry. I tried to apologize, but
she just looked at me with her sad eyes as if to
say: "How could you? You 're just like everybody
else."

I felt terrible afterwards, even worse than I
had when I received the critical note. I began to
question whether I was really helping any of the
kids I was working with. Maybe they were just per-
forming for me in the sessions but nothing was ever
changing. And with this precious kid —the mother
i sn't happy, the teacher isn't happy, and now she is
miserable too.

I experienced such remorse and feelings of
failure. I'm not good enough. I 'm not sensitive or
skilled enough. I should have known what to do. I
should have trusted myself more. I not only failed
this little girl, but I failed myself.

I could have been better. I should have been
better. My whole life A 's were never enough; they
had to be A + 's. 1 can feel good about myself as
l ong as I'm just with myself. When I feel judged by
others, I feel like a failure. I know I take things
awfully personal. I feel so responsible for everyone
and everything.

This new clinician's way of processing the case, reviewing her
conduct, and berating herself is typical not only of neophytes but
also of the veterans who lose sight of what is within their power
to control.

Lapses in Skill

Beginners' mistakes not only involve trusting your own intuition but extend to the basic helping skills. Beginning therapists act quite differently from experienced practitioners in the execution of most interventions. Whereas early in our careers we are likely to lose clients because of our awkward, unpolished efforts, practice almost makes perfect as years go by.

It is always gratifying to observe interns conducting interviews—not only because it reminds us how far we have come, but because we are reminded how effective even the most primitive interventions can be. Despite their imprecision in language, their stilted, nervous voice, their hesitation, their superficial focus, the beginner, the paraprofessional, even the parent who underwent a few hours of training can be remarkably effective using active listening skills. And when we observe the benefits of simple reflections of feeling, we realize once again that in our evolution toward more sophisticated strategies we may have abandoned precisely those techniques that are the most effective.

In the martial arts, for example, the advanced practitioner learns mostly through teaching introductory courses that review the basics of balance, posture, breathing, concentration, efficiency, and precision of movement. These principles from Tai Chi or Tae Kwan Do are exactly comparable to those we learn in the early practice of therapy —that is, to focus on our internal state (mood, attitude, mind free of distractions) and on our external form and attending behavior.

When we turn our attention to the specific therapeutic skills, and especially how they are bungled by novices, we begin to monitor our own rudimentary behavior. Most transcripts and videotapes of an intern would reveal an invaluable inventory of errors:

- Distracting mannerisms or facial expressions
- Poor attending skills and eye contact
- Difficulty following and focusing the direction of the client's statements
- The use of close-ended questions and an interrogative style that puts the client on the defensive

- Frequent interruptions of the client's natural stream of expression
- Noting surface messages of the client's verbalizations rather than deeper-level messages
- Relying exclusively on the content of communications rather than affect or process
- Using excessive self-disclosure and inappropriately putting the focus on oneself
- Exaggerated passivity in therapeutic style
- Difficulty tolerating silence
- Appearing unduly cold, aloof, and wooden in appearance
- Appearing too friendly, seductive, and informal
- Being aggressive or punitive in confrontations

Being aware of such basic blunders can help the beginner to remain vigilant during sessions with clients and thereby correct behavior that obviously impedes therapeutic progress.

Timing

Comedians often say that timing is everything. This statement holds true for the practice of therapy as well. New to the profession, beginners are not sensitive to the rhythm and pace of the therapeutic process. They err to either extreme, intervening too soon or waiting too long.

Ray began the initial session by describing his depression and despair. In her eagerness to find a source for the depression (and thereby a solution), Sue, the therapist, encouraged Ray to tell his life history. He related that his mother drank a great deal while he was growing up and said he felt like an outsider in the family and later in school. He had been divorced and had remarried . but Sue was no longer listening. Having specialized in her training program in treating substance abuse, Sue was certain that Ray 's depression emanated from growing up in an alcoholic family. With excitement, she began to hone her diagnosis and did not allow Ray to complete his story. The session ended with Sue reassuring Ray that once the issue of alcoholism was examined, he would surely feel better. But Ray did not return for another appointment. Sue had jumped to conclusions by not waiting for his full disclosure. She was unable to assess what was most critical to the client.

Jack wanted his client to like him and to feel comfortable in therapy. His client, Mary Ann, sought therapy because she was experiencing episodes of intense anxiety characterized by hyperventilation, dizziness, sweating, and eventual panic. Wanting to obtain a complete history, Jack spent the first four sessions questioning Mary Ann about her life. He was sure that she liked him because she complimented him each time they met and showed up early for all his appointments. Early one morning Jack received a frantic call from Mary Ann 's husband wanting t o know what to do. She was shaking and shivering in bed and could not move. Too late was Jack 's attention drawn to Mary Ann 's chief concern.

Both beginning therapists got caught in their own agendas. Their misguided sense of what was important clouded their abil- i t y to listen to what the client was saying. Being certain of a diagnosis without hearing the full story, or not attending to what is most pressing and critical to the client, are extreme ex ⁻ amples on the continuum of mistimed intervention. It is often not so much a matter of knowing what to say that challenges t herapists, beginner or veteran, but **when** to say it.

Fear of Confrontation

Wanting to be liked by the client is a frequent desire of beginning therapists. For if one is liked, the client will certainly return week after week, thus giving evidence of the beginner's success. New therapists, therefore, in their search for approval, often avoid setting limits with clients. Here are a few cases in point.

Bob 's client did not pay for the first few sessions. Bob did not want to confront the client for fear he might terminate t herapy, so he encouraged him to continue to come and said t hey could work out the finances later. Bob reasoned that it was more important for the client to be there working on recovery from cocaine addiction than for him to address the issue of money. When the client could not use payment as a way to avoid therapy, he quickly found another excuse, and within six weeks left treatment.

Ellen wanted the therapist to rearrange the therapy room each week in preparation for her session. This included moving a chair, turning off overhead lighting, and turning a desk clock away from her view. The therapist innocently agreed and each week got the room ready for Ellen 's session. Next she decided t hat she wanted a different day for her sessions. The therapist obliged. Ellen wondered if she could call the therapist at home "just when I need to . " The therapist agreed. The requests con - t i nued. And each time, in the interest of pleasing the client and avoiding confrontation , the therapist submitted to the demands. Within three months Ellen stopped coming to therapy. When contacted by the therapist, she said she had not gotten very much out of her sessions and she would not be coming back.

Clients often come to therapy expecting the therapist to acquiesce to their every whim . Beginning therapists tend to ac- cede to these demands in the interest of avoiding confronta - t i ons and preserving the therapeutic relationship. They worry t hat they might upset clients and drive them away. Sarah is a shy, sensitive, young therapist with a soft voice and gentle man - ner. She prizes acceptance and shows a high tolerance for behav- ior that might frustrate other colleagues. Always ready with an excuse why a client failed to show up or came late or did not pay or is stuck in a certain pattern , Sarah passively plods t hrough each therapeutic session. Feeling terror when chal- lenged by a client, Sarah would never consider challenging back. A virtual doormat for a client's attack or mistreatment, Sarah goes blithely along under the guise of acceptance, session after session. Some clients remain with her; their pathology continues t o flourish. Others, wanting to be challenged, wanting limits, de- part. But in Sarah 's belief system, there is no problem here. What- ever the client needs to do is of foremost importance for her. Thus all pathology is rationalized and inadvertently perpetuated .

When Life Messages Interfere

When we begin to explore the vulnerability of beginning practitioners, we often find that their therapeutic failures resonate with life messages they carry about themselves. Annie, a recovering alcoholic, works as a therapist in a residential substance abuse facility. As a child she constantly attempted to relieve her m other 's depression but was never successful. As an adult Annie chooses needy men to care for but has never felt successful at changing them either. The underlying theme for Annie has been "if only I had done more ."

Enter Roger, a needy alcoholic who has returned to the substance abuse facility and is assigned to Annie because his previous therapist is no longer on the staff. Annie finds herself with a client who is reminiscent of her mother and former boyfriends ' patterns of relapse and sets about fervently to instruct him in what he needs to do to get well. At some level Annie knows that she is not attending to other dynamics presented by the client. It is uppermost in her mind to save him and, in so doing, demon-strate that this time, finally, she has done enough. To her dismay, Roger relapses shortly after discharge from the facility.

For Annie, failure is "when you don 't take care of some-one well enough ." But now Annie wonders, "Why did I refuse t o see that my own issues were involved here ? " Annie 's acknowl-edgment and exploration of her failure allows her to recognize it as a potential block in her therapy with clients. By so doing, she becomes sensitive to its presence and commits herself to change. Thus Annie is paving the way for more effective therapy.

Linda was able to adapt to the obstacles presented in her family and later in school. Transferring from a nonchallenging high school to a private school stands out in Linda 's memory as an obstacle she overcame solely because "I learned how to play t he game." Unlike her previous school, the private school placed a strong emphasis on academics. Although Linda had moved from social success to academic excellence, she still had a feeling of academic incompetence. In Linda 's clinical work, a pervasive theme is "I don 't know enough; I'm pretending to be some-one I'm not . " In Linda 's life, when she can figure out the rules of the game, she plays it well. In the therapeutic process, how-ever, the rules of the game are in flux and not so easily deline-ated. Linda feels an urgent need to discover exactly what is going on in therapy so she can prove herself competent.

Margie vividly remembers accidentally bringing home her

friend 's perfect report card along with her less exemplary one. She recalls her mother 's outburst when comparing her marks with her friend 's distinctive record and the power of the message so vehemently delivered: "You should do better ! " In response to this recurrent theme, Margie moves through life striving for perfection and high achievement. When confronted with t herapeutic failure, a concept foreign to Margie until she began clinical work, her first thoughts place full responsibility square on herself: "I should have done better ! "

Annie 's concern with not doing enough, Linda 's focus on not knowing enough, Margie's striving for perfection —all are examples of messages introjected early in life that undermine our therapeutic effectiveness. We are, therefore, challenged to reflect upon our own life failures and the powerful messages t hat may be embedded within each of us. For in these messages may be the seeds of our fears of failure as adults and as therapists, and the concomitant promise of transformation that self-knowledge can provide.

Sometimes therapists are faced with an issue they have not yet confronted in their own lives. Yvonne, a young therapist, was faced with a client suffering from terminal cancer. Having never been touched by death , she felt like a robot with this client, nodding and saying "all the right things," yet inside she felt emotionally detached from what was occurring. It was t oo frightening to feel, to acknowledge the meaning of death , to let herself know that she would, one day, be confronting death in her own world.

Jack is in a marriage that brings little pleasure, yet he is a religious man, so divorce is not an option he would consider. In counseling a young couple having marital problems, Jack finds himself tacitly encouraging a separation. He wants the husband t o do what he himself is unwilling to do. He wants to make hap - pen in therapy something he would not make happen in his own life.

At times, even the most experienced therapists avoid con - fronting the damage they may unwittingly be causing during the t herapeutic hour. Behind closed doors, with only the client as witness, we may selfishly do our own psychological work or protect our own ego at our client's expense.

Not Listening to One's Intuition

Beginners, in their insecurity, seek supervision and advice on how best to work with their clients. They attribute weight and significance to the suggestions of their mentors and eagerly t r y to implement them . For in their desire to find the answer, t o help their clients resolve their concerns, they sometimes do not heed their own intuition. Indeed many beginners admit, "I fail when I'm not true to myself."

Each time Don was in session with Rita, a teenage client who reminded him of his adolescent daughter, he felt anger welling up inside. At some level he knew that what he was feeling related more to his domestic difficulties than to the young client sitting with him. Yet even so he chose to ignore his own inner voice and moved ahead with the treatment plan he and his supervisor had developed. This was Don 's first adolescent client. If he did well, his supervisor would be duly impressed, not to mention the girl's parents and teachers who were experiencing so much difficulty with her. Even with Rita 's resistance and Don 's rising anger, he plunged ahead, conscientiously implementing the treatment plan, yet all the while continuing to discount his own feelings. When the moment arrived that Don could no longer bury his anger, he exploded —not in supervision but in session with Rita. This shocking event terminated therapy and caused reverberations with all those parties Don had so wanted to impress. In reviewing the case with his supervisor, Don came to realize that with such an intense outward focus, he had not considered himself or valued the well of internal information waiting to be tapped .

Like a compass, there is an inner sense that helps point t he therapeutic direction, yet many neophytes, like Don , ignore what these voices tell them . They are launched out of the present and caught up in pleasing the referring professional, t he court, the client's family, the probation officer, a colleague. Visions of accolades and promotion fill their imagination. With applause ringing in their ears, they march ahead without consulting their most important resource—their own inner wisdom.

Lack of Confidence

When beginning any new endeavor, one usually suffers from too little or too much confidence. The former results in a weak will and tentative spirit; the latter can lead to unnecessary risk and bungled efforts. It is safe to say that most failures by t herapy interns are caused by the extremes on this continuum .

Pamela is a tentative and passive woman , recently divorced, who launched a career as a therapist after serving time as a depen - dent wife and mother. She was not used to being taken seriously by her adolescent children who did not listen to her, her ex-hus- band who continued to be abusive, and especially the ghost of her alcoholic father who used to beat her mercilessly as a child. Pamela found even steady eye contact to be a burden. Her voice was soft, her manner sheepish. Her whole being communicated t his tentative nature, and although she was quite loving, skilled, and well-meaning, her clients abandoned ship in droves. Appar- ently they found it difficult to trust in the competence of some- one who had so little faith in herself. Pamela did not even bother to learn how to fake that she knows what she is doing.

This beginner embodied almost all the undesirable traits associated with therapists who constantly fail. She was so in- secure that her so-called quiet strength became completely camouflaged. She dreaded every session as a supreme test of her basic worth. She exhibited a pessimistic, failing attitude , and her vocabulary was checkered with doubt —her favorite expres- sions were "I think so " or "I don 't know ." Pamela's cases rou - t i nely ended in defeat because she was utterly convinced she had no power to heal. Not surprisingly, she never quite made it t hrough her training experience and eventually found work else- where. What is most instructive about Pamela's manner is not her appalling lack of confidence, but how representative she is of those therapists who indirectly cause their failures by their self-sabotaging attitudes.

Impatience

In wanting to see results, new therapists are eager for evi- dence of their impact on clients. They want to see proof that t hey are succeeding. Unfamiliar with the wide range of clients' rhythms and processes, they move ahead with speed and dis‑ patch at the first sign of an identifiable problem . As soon as t hey have a grasp of some dynamic they can point to, they in‑ tervene, impatient to "get started ," to be active, to cause some‑ t hing to happen . One trainee said, "I want to heat it up real quick and get to the meat of things." What he really meant was t hat he needs immediate evidence that he is making a differ‑ ence. He thinks it is better for something to happen , even if it may ultimately be contraindicated , than for nothing to occur.

Believing they know better than the client—and not trust‑ ing in the client's ability to discover for himself or herself—new t herapists interfere in the client's own process of growth and learning. The therapist tells the client something that she is not yet ready to hear; the therapist offers a solution before the cli‑ ent is given the opportunity to consider options; the therapist races blithely ahead expecting the client to follow the lead rather than fitting the pace to the subtle rhythms of each per‑ son. It is a discordant melody of syncopated movements lacking in harmony, in fluidity, in connection .

Impatience seems to be the centerpiece of the beginner's struggle. Lacking the sensitivity of experience, eager to succeed, believing they know more than they really do, neophytes leap i nto dark waters causing ripples that affect their client's growth as well as their own clinical effectiveness.

Innocence

In their collection of therapeutic blunders, Robertiello and Schoenwolf (1987) report the case of a young therapist who had not yet developed an appropriate detachment and im ‑ munity from a particularly seductive client. The client had elic‑ it ed in the therapist (just as she had in a string of others), a mix ‑ t ure of anger and attraction so intense that he felt speechless. "In essence, she had put this therapist in a double bind: If he responded to her seductiveness, she would have contempt for him, and if he did not respond, she would be insulted " (p. 24).

Such a situation could easily arise for therapists who be‑

come so hypnotized by a client's games that they fail to hold t heir projective feelings in check. In the preceding case, the t herapist realized it was appropriate to confront the client re-garding her blatant sexual innuendos, but his angry tone drove her away. As often happens when we are uncomfortable with a client, he helped her to leave. Variations on this theme include prematurely declaring a client cured or putting up a cold screen to drive the client away.

Mistaking the Label for the Person

It is characteristic for beginners to feel uncertain of their knowledge and skills. Fear, a volatile resident in their hearts, gets sparked when a case is presented to them with a threaten – ing label—"paranoid personality," "anorexic," "borderline." What leaps into their consciousness is a desperate attempt to re-trieve everything they have ever read, heard, or learned about this particular pathology, as if to arm themselves against an overpowering enemy. When therapists are geared toward con – fronting the client as a strong opposing force, they have already prevented themselves from receiving the client with full accep-t ance and positive regard. They have already decided who the client is and what the treatment must be. They may have dealt with their own fear, but their stance of determination and cer-t ainty cannot help but evoke fear in the unsuspecting client. The therapeutic relationship, no longer a partnership, begins as an adversarial contest between two persons.

The First Taste of Failure

One beginner compared her experience of failure to a football game. By dint of great effort, she is able to nudge the ball of progress five, maybe ten , yards toward the goal. Suddenly a failure knocks her back thirty to forty yards. She feels shaken, exhausted, and in despair. Another novice experiences failure as a hairline fracture in the terrain of therapy that feels to her like an earthquake.

From these descriptions, it is clear that failure makes a

profound impact on therapists experiencing it for the first ti me. It is alarming; it stops them dead ; it generates aftershocks t hat disturb their entire world. Self-doubt becomes persistent and pervasive. It generalizes from this specific client to quest i oning one 's effectiveness with every client and continues to erode the person 's sense of self until he or she wonders about his or her very worth as a person. Indeed, failure can be poisonous if neophyte therapists are unable to use it as a learning experience and place it in perspective. They can be assisted in this task by watching the way we veterans confront our failures and the positive outcome that can result from self-examination.

As beginners, we had many lessons to learn. Presumably we learned them well and have not knowingly repeated our early mistakes. On the other hand, we may now be complacent, our senses dulled by the busy routine and security that a full caseload affords, our apparent success making it difficult to admit, if only in our deepest whisperings, our own failures. Re-experiencing the mistakes of beginners can help us recognize our own vulnerability and give us a new respect for basic therapeutic wisdom.

6

How Client's
and Therapist's Fears
of Failure Influence
Each Other

While there is indeed a difference between the mistakes of a beginner and those of a veteran , both share a vulnerability to t he emotionally charged issues of the client. During any given session there is a running dialogue within the minds of client and therapist in which each responds to the other, both inter- nally and externally. Not only do we talk to one another, but we talk to ourselves during this interaction, responding to ideas and feelings within us.

Clients speak not only to us about their insecurities, vul- nerabilities, and terror, but with us in the sense that we inter- nalize their messages on multiple levels. Although a major part of our mind is concentrating on the helping role, there is always a part of us held in reserve that is personalizing much of what is occurring in sessions. All the while the client is shivering in an- t i cipation of risking, failing, and being judged harshly, we are doing much of the same ourselves. In effect, client and therapist trigger for one another their own respective fears.

The client confides his sense of despondency and hope - lessness. Not only is he a failure as a father, a husband , and a businessman, but he cannot even succeed in therapy —where even losers feel like winners. Week after week he only slips deeper i nto his depression. And all the while he is blaming himself as a hopeless client, the therapist cannot help but feel her own exas- peration and apprehension: "Maybe it 's me. Perhaps if I knew more, or was brighter, or better trained, or more patient, or more loving, sessions would not be proceeding so dismally."

Defenses slip into gear. For both of us. Just as we remind ourselves that we cannot be responsible for matters outside our control, that the client must decide, at his own pace, when he is ready to improve, just when we are feeling a little better, the client changes tactics and goes on the offensive. We have no pati ence when he insists on blaming bad luck and a poor business climate for his plight. We confront his excuses and then, during a moment of reflection, realize we have been doing the same thing.

Reciprocal Influences in Therapy

Randi sat staring straight ahead or looking down , eyes always cast away from her therapist. Her feet were in constant motion , tapping some anxious rhythm known only to her. Her hands were gripped firmly together, her knuckles were pale and tight. Bandages covered an area on her hands where she had cut herself in a moment of self-destructive rage. Despite her efforts t o appear under control, she was shivering. Over and over she repeated the same verbal messages: "I'm fine. Leave me alone! There 's no hope ." Whatever the therapist said was met with re- j ection -each time the therapist dipped into her reservoir and brought forth another idea, a door slammed shut.

At each rejection the therapist felt her chest tighten and her frustration mount. She felt desperate to make contact with Randi, to free her from her depression, to rescue her from her pain. But the more the therapist searched and struggled, the more uneasy she became. Randi later told her that she felt like a failure in therapy —the therapist's frustration signaled her that she was not okay, that she was not meeting the therapist's ex - pectations. The more frustrated the therapist became and the harder she battled her fear of failure, the more convinced Randi became that it was she who had failed. Each of them was caught up with her own fear of failure; a deteriorating cycle was being perpetuated .

And the cycle continues. Therapist influences client.

Client, in turn, affects therapist. Both of us sometimes end up jabbing at raw nerve endings. This reciprocal influence between partners in therapy has been seen as the greatest hardship and yet the most spectacular benefit of our chosen profession (Kottler, 1986). As the client risks, grows, changes as a result of heated dialogue and intense intimacy, so too does the therapist. And as the client faces his or her failures, so must we examine our own fears. Hobson (1985, p. 261) writes in his journal about this interactive effect and how we all attempt to avoid the darkness of failure—first in our clients and then in ourselves:

It is M onday morning. Washing day. Su e 's voice is dull and monotonous.

"It is all a waste of time   . we just go around in circles   . n othing changes   . j u s t   t he same. Now Jim has dropped me. . .   . Oh, I know , I know, I made him reject me, but knowing is no damn use. We were talking like this twelve years ago . . . you are fed up with it too.   .   And then I give you hell ringing you up ten times over the weekend   .   a nd t aking those pills   . sleeping in your garden and t hrowing stones through your windows.   ... I can't cope . . . I really can 't cope   . I 'm no good. You are fed up too. I know you are."

Sue is right. I am fed up. but that is to put it too mildly. Psychotherapy is no good. I can 't cope. Sue 's vicious attacks have gouged out m y inside and all the weekend m y fam ily life has been in chaos. Today my wife has a big wash, and I have to get through a day o f difficult interviews and intermina - ble committees. She has failed and feels that she herself is a failure. I have failed. I am a failure.

Just as clients respond to our upbeat attitude , our cheerful resolve to help them , we in turn respond to their despair.

When they feel forlorn, hopeless, despondent, in spite of our best efforts to ward off these feelings, we are nevertheless affected profoundly. And as we resonate with their feelings of failure, we sometimes experience, once again, our own dormant fears.

A Dialogue

The following interaction between therapist and client, t herapist and himself, brings alive the very real consequences of facing failure every day. There are not just the combative strug-gles with clients who undermine our most helpful efforts, de - fending themselves by attacking our sense of competence, but t he malignant fears and failures of their lives that are all too fa- miliar to our own experience.

The Client. Lori is an extremely bright, sensitive, and attractive

young woman of twenty-four. Although she wears no makeup, lets her hair fall naturally, and wears only jeans and sweaters, she is quite beautiful. She has no notion how she appears to others. When she looks in the mirror she sees only imperfec-ti ons: Her legs could be longer, her cheekbones higher, her eyes more sparkly, her hair a different texture . This is in spite of making no effort whatsoever to adorn herself in clothes or ac-cessories that might be more flattering to her athletic and grace-ful frame. She thus gives herself an excuse why someone might not notice her. Inside she feels like a hag, a complete failure as a woman.

Although Lori graduated from a major university with a grade point average of 3.8, scored in the 98 th percentile on her Graduate Record Exam , and is currently a doctoral student in psychology, she considers herself fairly average or even below average in intelligence. In explaining her accomplishments she says she is just lucky, a good test taker, or a hard worker. If you t hen compliment her on being a hard worker, she will deny her earlier admission and claim she does not work nearly as hard as she should. Lori reeks of failure.

The Therapist. Lori's therapist, Ted, is an attractive man   al-

t hough he shares her lifelong feelings of physical inadequacy. Of slight build and no particular athletic gifts, he suffered on the playground as a child, always the last to be chosen for any team sport. As an adult he sought refuge in noncompetitive, solitary pursuits—bicycling, skiing—activities in which he would not feel j udged by others.

Like his client, Ted felt stupid most of his life. His parents, teachers, and peers viewed him as a nice person but un remarkable in any way —destined for middle management in a medium -size company. He rebelled against his family 's and t eachers ' modest expectations for him, their judgments that he was lazy, slow, and without promise. While in the early years he only confirmed his image as a failure, consistently received barely passing grades, dropped fly balls in right field, and kept t o himself, in college he blossomed. After this slow marathon of mediocrity, he sprinted hard during his training years and, much t o his surprise, became known as an exceptional scholar and talented clinician. Nobody remembers any longer the shy, inept failure of a kid. Nobody , that is, except Ted himself.

Their Interaction. And now the client and therapist close them

selves together in a quiet room , Lori who appears smart and beautiful and pretends she is dumb and ugly, Ted who pretends he is bright and charming yet feels inadequate and shy. They size each other up warily, each alone with personal thoughts and fears, both wishing desperately not to disappoint the other. Lori is confiding her despair, hopelessness, eternal depression. But t he therapy does not seem to be helping. She apologizes. She has always failed at everything she tried. This is no different. Pause. Sob. Silence.

Ted attempts to dispute her recollections. "You failed at everything? Everything ? Not once have you ever succeeded at

anything? How, after all, did you get into graduate school? "

Lori slips further into her despondency as she stonily averts her eyes. The therapist starts to panic as he thinks to him self: "I 'm losing her and it 's my fault. I 've got to convince her she has succeeded in something, but no matter what I try, I can 't reach her ." He begins several times to demonstrate some elusive point he can no longer remember. The client waits with defiant calm and almost dares him to convince her she is any-t hing more than a loser. In exasperation, his eyes flee the room and settle on a tall oak tree outside the window ; it stands barren and alone on a March day. Relief floods over him as he finally settles on a new tack.

"Can you see that tree growing out in the field?"

Lori seems preoccupied, but she decides to indulge the overeager therapist. She replies listlessly: "No, of course not ."

"Then does that mean it isn't growing just because it is happening slower than your awareness?"

Feeling smug and satisfied with his clever maneuver, Ted t hinks he has averted disaster. She seems to understand . But what a short-lived victory! For in his heart Ted knows she will once again return to her deep feelings of inadequacy, igniting doubts within the therapist as well. He wonders to himself why he feels so hooked by this case, why he is trying so hard to con – vince them both they are making progress.

Lori, as well, seems reflective. "Gosh, this poor guy is doing so much to help me and I'm always disappointing him. I wonder what he 's thinking ? "

The therapist's seemingly patient smile covers his own in– ner turmoil. "It 's bad enough that I'm letting her down , but what will her father think? He 's some big-shot neurologist and so far he 's been pretty impressed with me. I thought he might start referring some of his patients if I did a good job with his daughter. But if she gives up, he 'll think it 's my fault.   . But he 's a doctor. He should be used to thinking of failures as some– t i mes inevitable.   . Maybe this w on 't reflect on my compe – t ence after all.   . But if she sees someone else   . God, how can I be so vain and self-centered! This poor young woman is hurting, I can 't seem to do much to help, and all I can think about is how this affects me. How can I avoid feeling like a fail– ure just because she does ? "

Lori finally responds. "I keep looking at that tree out t here, and you 're right, of course, I probably am doing better even if I feel pretty much the same. But that tree reminds me so much of myself. I mean, it 's so plain and lonely."

Ted 's stomach tightens and he clenches his teeth. His mind continues racing. "Maybe this is all part of her sickness.

She doesn 't really want to get better. She likes failing. Hell, she's had enough practice! Now she 's even hooking me into her stuff. I feel like a failure too. Maybe I can use this somehow . If I can pull myself out, maybe she 'll follow ."

Lori interrupts her therapist's inner dialogue. If she cannot make herself feel better, maybe she can at least help somebody else. Always in character. Giving of herself, even in her own therapy, especially with this person who has become what she so much wishes to be.

"But you have helped me. I mean, where else could I t urn ? If I let my professors or classmates in on how moody I get, they 'll diagnose me in a second, and then they 'll relegate me to that special place—half empathetic /half condescending — t hey reserve for all 'patients .' Certainly I know this is all up to me. It 's not your fault I'm so uncooperative ."

Ted considers the statement suspiciously, looking for the t r ap, and then realization settles on his face. "She 's trying to let me off the hook . The fact of the matter is I've been too t i mid in my interventions. I've been so cautious not wanting to mess things up that I haven 't risked confronting her at all."

"Lori, it has just occurred to me that in my work with you I have been uncharacteristically cautious. I have been re- l uctant to confront you at all for fear you might fall apart. But I just realized that I would be accepting your image of yourself as a human wreck, and I certainly don 't agree with that assess- ment. In fact, I think you like feeling the way you do and enjoy all the excuses you 've collected for remaining the same. And I t hink, unconsciously, you are doing everything you can to sabo- t age the therapy. You want us to fail."

Lori shows anger, then incredulity, but she refuses to respond. She imperceptibly shakes her head and looks out the window toward the tree. Ted begins to question the wisdom of his i ntervention. Maybe he was too direct. Could he be that far off t he mark? He wonders why it is so important to be right. Ted l ooks across the room , sees Lori shivering, and feels censured and shamed. Reluctant to be wrong yet again, he does not know what to say or do next. The back of his shirt feels wet. He can- not get comfortable in his chair.

Then Lori explodes. "You know what kind of pressure I'm under! My father is a doctor, Mother is a lawyer—I can't ever seem to please them. Nothing is ever good enough. Oh, t hey never criticize me openly, but I can tell they expect more. Even my decision to be a psychologist is less than a real doctor. My dad says they don't really do anything except blame other doctors for giving people too many drugs."

Ted reflects in silence. "Maybe she's right. I know if I could have handled the chemistry courses, or gotten accepted to medical school, I'd be a 'real doctor' instead. Well, maybe that's not true. But then why do I feel so defensive?" At last he speaks. "Well, Lori, what's the connection between the way your parents have treated you and the way you act today?"

"I can't stand the thought of anyone judging me. I keep dropping out —of relationships, commitments, anything —just t o avoid being judged. I put myself down so bad that nobody could ever hurt me worse. There's nothing anyone could say to me I haven't thought of first."

The Implications. A conversation and inner dialogue such as   this could crop up anywhere, if not in this extreme form, then in a more diluted manner. There is no doubt that many of the fears vibrating within our clients are also harbored within each of us. Their sense of uncertainty and inadequacy, their distorted self-portraits, their constant need for explanation, for control, evoke familiar themes which we rail fervently against, in our own efforts to avoid the demons in our own psyches.

And so this interplay of client and therapist affecting one another's thoughts, feelings, and responses continues. If we are alert, it can become a resource, a tool for facilitating growth within ourselves and for the client. Left unheeded, however, it can distort the relationship and destroy the valuable interaction between client and therapist.

Disclosures of Failure

In confronting our own imperfections we become better equipped to help others cope with their own. Each and every ti me we experience failure in our sessions, unresolved personal struggles can be easily triggered. By consulting with others, sharing our bungled cases, we are better able to deal with them , learn from them , and ultimately come to terms with ourselves.

Since one of the stated purposes of this book is to bring failure out of the closet, to invite more open dialogue among professionals when things go wrong, we consider the case descriptions by a number of professionals—obscure or famous, veterans or beginners—to be the core of our message. But we can hardly expect either the reader, our colleagues, or the many clinicians who contributed their experiences to this project to expose their greatest failures unless we are willing to do so ourselves. Just as we asked graduate students, beginning and ex - perienced therapists, theoreticians, and prominent practitioners t o discuss their failures, it is time for us to present, with reluc-t ance and shame (as many of our colleagues must have felt), the following encounters. These incidents demonstrate how the client 's (or trainee 's) fear of failure affects the emotional life of t he therapist—which, in turn , has a reciprocal impact on the client 's continued fear and apprehension.

Diane 's Failure as a Supervisor. While clinical
failures   have   cer-t ainly been instructive for me, here I wish to relate an experience from supervision that exemplifies my struggle with dis-t orted self-perceptions and unrealistic expectations, its impact upon the trainee, and the learning and change that resulted.

A few minutes after completing the last session of a course I was teaching, I was called on the intercom by the academic vice-president. I was to come to her office. Peeling exhilarated by the final seminar and rather pleased with myself, I walked into her office to find seated there one of the students 1 had been supervising throughout the semester. I was half-expecting words of praise, but my perspective quickly changed t o one of apprehension as I noted the solemnity and tension t hat filled the room .

I took a chair across from the student and as I looked at her face and into her eyes, I could see she was boiling with anger. As she glared back at me, her eyes boring through my body, I felt the heat of her rage. It was so intense, I found my - self edging my chair back to protect myself. I began by saying,

"It looks as if you have something to say to me ." And as soon as I did, her fury poured forth. In a loud voice she berated me, t elling me how incompetent I had been as a supervisor, how I had not offered enough guidance or direction, how she did not value me at all as supervisor, as teacher, not even as a human being. In fact, she screamed, she had been doing so poorly at her internship that she was now on probation .

While she had not been a particularly responsive student, I had seen no indication of her apparent distress, for in sessions with me she had reported positive results and disclosed very lit- tl e difficulty. I was therefore shocked by her revelation and t aken aback by the strong feelings that were bombarding me. Never before had I been confronted with such force and anger in such an intensely venomous manner. I felt myself shrink in t he chair and grasp its arms tightly with both hands. I planted my feet firmly on the floor almost to prevent myself from being blown away. My breathing was shallow and rapid and my stom - ach knotted in a tight ball. I realized my thinking had narrowed. My one great need was to protect myself from this assault.

Foremost in my mind was a simple thought: " It 's not me, i t 's her ." I felt a coldness come over me as I fought to distance myself from her. It seemed that the more emotional she was, t he more aloof I became. I looked to my colleague to defend me, to support me, to offer a litany of my strengths, but she seemed to be unaware of the pain I was experiencing and was focused instead on helping the student. I heard myself say, "I don 't like the way you are speaking to me. I will not take any more ! " Yet I felt glued to the chair, immobilized, and to my surprise on the verge of tears. The confrontation ended with an agreement that the student would transfer to another supervisor for the remainder of the academic year.

Feeling both relieved and defeated , I left the room and made my way back to my office. As soon as I closed the door, I began to sob. I was startled by my reaction. Certainly I had been confronted and criticized before, but never with such vehemence. I saw myself as having failed so badly as a super- visor that the student no longer wanted to work with me. In my complacency I had failed to notice her distress and to acknowledge my own inadequacy in helping her. It was as if there had been a tacit agreement between us: She would not voice her fears and tell me how inadequate she felt ("What if I don 't have what it takes to be a therapist? ") and I would perpetuate the charade by not acknowledging my fear of being unable to help her ("What if I'm caught making a mistake ? ").

The very foundation of my being seemed shattered by this experience, and I felt compelled to make sense of it and come to terms with it. What had been shaken was a sense of my - self as being nearly perfect, as an exceptional supervisor and t eacher, as being gifted in my ability to work effectively with even the most difficult students and supervisees. Now I needed t o confront this obsolete image and create a more honest one.

The ride home in my car that day was long and painful. I found myself alternating between crying and distracting myself with whatever positive thoughts I could muster and then crying again. I came home to an empty house. My husband was attend - ing a conference out of town and 1 was thus unable to solicit his support by telling my woeful tale, building my case, and dem - onstrating how blameless I was and how good I really am. l was alone with my feelings, with my self.

I began to realize that I had been deceiving myself and had been an accomplice to the student's distorted view of her- self. We both had pretended that everything was progressing sat- isfactorily. When told she was on probation , her fears erupted and her rage spilled onto me. ("I'll blame you and then I w on 't have to examine myself.") When I was so unjustly accused   (or so I thought), I was guilty of using the same protective devices. (" It 's her, not me .")

For me this experience goes far beyond the question of competency. What became so apparent was how well I had pro - t ected myself from looking at my own frailties and imperfec- t i ons and how skillfully I found excuses to combat criticism. Even the colleagues with whom I had surrounded myself were a virtual cheering section. Was I as dishonest with them as they were with me? Were we all accomplices in self-deception?

It t ook the intensity of heated anger to pierce my armor, t o cause me to take a hard look at my well-developed defenses, t o accept my culpability, to be open to seeing the experience in a realistic light. I was able to acknowledge my own complacency in my work with this student and review what l   might have done differently in ways that might have been more useful. In so doing I was able to forgive myself for mistakes I had made.

I set about to reestablish a relationship with the student and renew my commitment to be honest and straightforward with her and with myself. My willingness to recognize my con − t r i bution to this fiasco encouraged her to do the same. Soon the distance and anger between us —each blaming the other for what t r uly lay within ourselves—was transformed into a working alli− ance from which we both benefited.

In all my interactions with clients, students, and super− visees, none to date has been more illuminating than this expe− rience of failure. In attempting to stave off her own fears of failure, the student had attacked my competence and thereby triggered my own fears of inadequacy. In my usual fashion I had mobilized all my resources and rallied to protect my ego. Un− fortunately it took this painful event to break through my wellconstructed layers of protection , to dispel my unrealistic beliefs, t o force me to see myself more honestly. Despite the distress of this experience, I had received a gift—a powerful reminder of my vulnerability and humanness.

Jeffrey 's Failure as a Therapist. It has been over six years   since   I last saw Arthur and I still do not feel very good about the way things ended, especially the way I conducted myself during the closing of our relationship. I suppose the fact that I still muse over the case and still feel remnants of frustration , anger, self-doubt, and incompetency does not say much for how I have handled myself since then. I usually pride myself on my ability t o let go of things I cannot do much about. Yet this case con − t i nues to haunt me.

Arthur approached me originally because of a failing mar− riage he could do little to salvage. His wife had made up her mind that things had progressed beyond repair. She felt mis− t r ustful and betrayed by Arthur and believed he was having an affair that he would not admit to. Therapy represented Arthur 's attempt to convince his wife that he would do anything to win her approval.

Arthur presented himself as a very earnest and sincere fellow. He was immediately forthright regarding his intentions and stated quite openly that he had never failed at anything in his life and certainly did not intend to start now, especially since t h e stakes involved losing his infant child and wife. He would do almost anything to show his good faith and be given another chance.

Although I usually prefer weekly appointments so that clients have sufficient opportunity to reflect on the content of sessions and act, if indicated, on their insights, I made an excep - t i on in Arthur 's case for several reasons. He seemed very dis- t r aught and apprehensive and would profit from intensive support during this vulnerable stage. He was highly motivated and i mpatient to experience some relief of his symptoms. I liked Arthur a lot and really wanted to help him avoid his failure (never realizing that events would lead to my own). And (I am ashamed to admit) he claimed money was no object and he could easily afford my fees for sessions as often as I could fit him in.

After we had dispensed with the issue of money and the structural parameters of the treatment plan, he also encouraged me to open lines of communication with his wife 's therapist. He hoped that eventually conjoint work would be possible between t h e four of us. Since the other therapist was a prominent psy- chiatrist I had heard a lot about, I was doubly pleased that I had an excuse to call her —not only to get background information t hat might be helpful in working with Arthur but also to make an impression on this female authority figure. (Was 1 trying to win my deceased m other 's approval who never knew me as an adult?)

Well, the seeds of disaster in this fiasco had all been sown. Blissfully ignorant of my miscalculation on a number of scores, I proceeded. A lengthy phone conversation ensued with the psy- chiatrist in which I tried hard to impress her —giving away in the process more than I intended. All I got from her was the advice t o collect my fees from Arthur in advance since she claimed he was a "sleazy deadbeat." In turn , I told her, in confidence, that t he reason Arthur was resisting his wife 's demands that he straighten himself out was because he was actually quite ambiv‑ alent as he had been having an affair with his wife 's best friend. I succeeded in impressing my esteemed colleague with this val‑ uable information —so much so that she shared the conversa‑ t i on with her client who in turn berated poor Arthur as soon as she got home.

For obvious reasons, my next session with Arthur did not go well. He raged at me for betraying his trust and accused me of violating his confidence. He would have no part of my ex ‑ cuses that I had only called the therapist at his request and how could I know she would let information from a professional con ‑ sultation slip out to her client. He demanded retribution and I was only too eager to comply. Arthur believed the least I could do was to see his girlfriend to explain the situation, and in what could only be described as a moment of temporary insanity, I agreed. While that session went well, I now found myself so far over my head I did not know where to go next. That was fine with Arthur, who knew exactly where he wanted to go next. He brought his wife to the subsequent session—and, in so many words, presented me as the bad influence who was sabotaging t heir marriage. His wife was so hostile toward me that Arthur escaped unscathed. In fact, from his point of view, things worked out perfectly: (1) His wife agreed to reconciliation, sav‑ ing Arthur from his dreadful failure; (2) he was able to continue seeing his girlfriend; and (3) true to his reputation as a "sleazy deadbeat," he refused to pay the bill for the thirty sessions we had met.

I had been had. I felt enraged. I wanted revenge. At least I wanted my fair payment for services rendered. But I also was filled with doubt. I was so confused that I was not even sure how I had messed things up, or even if I had. All I knew was t hat Arthur came in feeling like a failure and by the time he left, free of his burden , I had caught his symptoms.

I have tried every trick I know to overcome my feelings of inadequacy related to this case. I have repeatedly told myself t hat Arthur needed the therapy to fail. It even seems reasonable t hat he sabotaged things merely to avoid paying his bill; that would be in keeping with his character. I have asked myself why t his particular incident is so difficult for me to forget. I have sought counsel with several colleagues attempting to uncover the trigger for my troubles.

After years of reflection I conclude that the principal value of this failure was to teach me humility —to remind me of all the things I will never understand about myself or others. I deliberately did not pursue collection procedures to get paid. For one thing, I was afraid Arthur 's wife would sue me for some imagined malpractice. And I did not want to be in a position to defend myself when I felt such diffused guilt. But 1 also think I wanted to punish myself for misjudging this case so spectacu ⁻ larly—I did not deserve to be paid. I recall how hard I worked and how little I got from him in return, either in appreciation or compensation . And yet my interaction with Arthur taught me as much as any person alive. He still haunts me, and I imagine he will continue to do so in order that I may be reminded of the painful lessons learned under his tutelage.

In Retrospect

All three examples presented in this chapter —the dialogue of failure and our two disclosures—point to a complex, interac⁻ ti ve effect between client and therapist in the way each comes t o terms with personal vulnerability. It is our observation that t he struggle with failure, its avoidance, denial, and eventual ac⁻ ceptance, follows a parallel course that is both stimulated and retarded by exposure to the others in the therapeutic encoun ⁻ ter. Ideally, as the therapist improves in personal effectiveness, he or she becomes a model for how to deal with risks in life and t he aftermath of less than desirable results. Unfortunately , the realities of professional practice and daily life make it difficult for many of us to accept our failures and handle the emotional pain they bring.

This task would be a lot easier if those at the forefront of the field could be more frank about their own imperfections as well as discussing their strategies for coping with negative re⁻ sults. This is exactly the subject of the chapter that follows.

7

The Imperfections
of Prominent Practitioners

For years our field 's most prominent practitioners have been churning out research, books, conferences, workshops, all t estifying to the power and magic of their interventions. It is inspiring indeed to watch Minuchin work with a family, or Yalom run a group, or Ellis conduct an interview. Again and again peo – ple like Rogers, Peris, and May have demonstrated how effec‑ ti ve their strategies can be.

These wondrous demonstrations follow the tradition established by great therapists of the past who related stories of hopeless cases that were miraculously cured by brilliant diagnosis and treatment. As students we felt in awe of cases such as " Ratman " or "Anna O . " presented by Freud; they read like the fairy-tales with happy endings we used to hear as children. In his case of obsessional neurosis Freud declares: "One day the patient mentioned quite casually an event which I could not fail t o recognize as the exciting cause of his illness . " Uncanny clinical skill was soon being documented by Freud 's heirs, as well, who in their turn presented exemplary case studies (but a dearth of failures) to substantiate their theories.

In an anthology of such successes, we are exposed to Ad – l er's case of "Mrs. A .," Jung 's "Man with a Dream ," Rogers's "Case of Mrs. Oak ," Ellis's case of "The Black and Silver Masochist," Wolpe's "Case of Mrs. C .," Perls's "Case of Jane ," and Glasser's "Case of Aaron " (Wedding and Corsini, 1979). There is no doubt that these examples are immensely helpful in high‑ l i ghting how various theories operate during sessions, and they certainly attest to the remarkable skill of these practitioners.

107

There have been side effects in response to this habit, however, in that failure has been pushed further underground.

In our modern times, model films, videos, and audiotapes have been produced demonstrating the various approaches to t herapy at their best; they show the master therapist cutting t hrough the client's resistance, pinpointing the real presenting problems, resolving important issues, and still saving a few min - utes at the end to process what actually occurred. It is daunting t o the beginner and veteran alike to see such perfect examples of how therapy should be done. Indeed, such demonstrations have moved more than a few therapists to ask themselves: Don 't these people ever blow an interview? Don 't they ever say any - t hing stupid? Don 't they ever lose a client?

One of the reasons it has been so difficult to discuss ther- apy failures is because many of those at the forefront of the field have been more involved in advocating their particular viewpoint than in creating a unified concept of helping. If the most prominent clinicians and theoreticians do not discuss their failures, how are the rest of us ever to accept the regularity with which our own best efforts fall short?

We decided to enlist the help of exemplary therapists on t he subject of failure. We reasoned that if those who have the most to lose by way of sterling reputations were willing to dis- cuss their mishaps and mistakes, perhaps these honest disclosures would help other practitioners feel less alone in their imperfec- tions. Although these veterans are not immune to blundering, t hey often process their failures quite differently than beginners.

We invited these brave few to describe one experience with failure. We asked them to record their story on paper or t ape, paying particular attention to their own internal process during and after the episode. We were also interested in what t hey learned from the experience and how it has since affected t heir lives. We applaud the honesty and openness of James F. T. Bugental, Richard Fisch, Albert Ellis, Arnold Lazarus, Gerald Corey, and Clark Moustakas in presenting themselves in an im- perfect light so that the rest of us may learn from their mistakes and feel more willing to confront our own.

Bugental: "I Certainly Have Had Failures"

James Bugental has been a major force in relationship-oriented therapy for decades. His books, Challenges, o f Human-istic Psychology (1957), The Search fo r Existential Identity (1976), Psychotherapy and Process (1 9 7 8), and The Art o f the Psychotherapist (1987), emphasize the process of therapy and have become classic statements of the role that sensitivity, love, and intuition play in the therapeutic encounter. In his words:

"Every psychotherapy course is a failure and almost ever)' psychotherapy course is a success. Or to put it more ac‑curately: Nearly every psychotherapy course succeeds in some ways and fails in others. Of course, there are the extreme in‑stances in which therapy falls so short of what is needed that t he client commits suicide or some terrible act of violence. Less dramatically, there are also the extreme instances of major life changes which result in significant contributions to the arts, sci‑ences, or other fields. I would hazard, however, that even in these latter cases there were some failings in the work itself even t hough the overall product is so manifestly superlative.

"When the whole course of my work with certain pa‑ t i ents is reviewed, I certainly have had failures—by my own standards. Here are some examples.

"Bill was a young psychotherapist and group leader with a degree from an institution that was at best marginal in stan‑dards. He came to me for therapy because (it became evident) he thought it would be good to show on his resume that he had done so and because he wanted to 'see how you do it.' Under‑neath these superficial reasons, I think there was much need of deeper therapeutic efforts. I found myself disliking our work t ogether, annoyed with his pseudosophistication, and impatient with his feelings of superiority to his own clients. Not too sub‑ tl y I encouraged his withdrawing from therapy.

"I failed Bill because I would not make the investment needed to challenge him to the work he really needed. There was little success in our brief time together. I have the hope that t he limited but reasonably candid feedback I gave him at our last session may mix with other experiences within Bill and eventually lead to his grappling more maturely with his life.

"Nina was a wife and mother who had known periods of despondency all her life and who, when in such a mood , frequently provoked others into wrangles. After an initial period of our sparring and learning how to relate with each other, we were able to establish a firm alliance. Thereafter, she was faith ‐ ful in coming and in paying her account, she carried out my suggestions for using our hours, and she seemed to 'do therapy ' appropriately. Yet in three plus years there was no real change in her emotional issues.

"I failed Nina, although I'm not sure how. My best guess is that I misread the depth of her depressive character and there ‐ fore didn 't help her come to an adequate accommodation to it. Although limited, the successful aspects of our work were manifested in her taking more responsibility for her bouts of fury, l earning to set limits to her accessibility to an astonishingly bru ‐ t alizing family of origin, and becoming less likely to continue these patterns with her own children.

"You will have noticed that in both instances I speak of how I failed the client. This phrasing arises from my belief that it is my responsibility to try to provide a situation which the client can use to make significant life changes. I cannot, by any means, always do so. However, to say I failed these and other clients is not to adjudge myself a failure as a therapist. I know t hat I am not. It is to acknowledge that I am very human and t r uly limited.

"In my therapeutic failures—and perhaps those of other t herapists—the common denominator is, as I see it, the therapist's hesitation to invest as fully, to be as truly present, as the client needs. This can take many forms as my examples suggest. Life-changing psychotherapy is demanding of both participants. It is not to be accomplished only by skillful technique, sophis‐ t i cated theory, or scholarly detachment. Its medium is the lively alliance of two people in a struggle with the dark forces that de‐ stroy personal fulfillment and result in our being crippled and less than we might otherwise be.

"We fail our patients when we pull back from genuine investment in our work, when we hesitate to confront them for fear of their anger, their disappointment in us, or their taking flight. We fail them when we do not call on them for the greater investment (of time, emotion, money) needed to do the work for which they came to therapy. We fail them when we divert them from emotional outbursts, transference 'messiness,' or bluntly facing the ultimate insolubility of life. We fail them when we refuse to take responsibility for our own neurotic distortions.

"When we talk about the struggles that are the reality of life-changing psychotherapy, we confuse our thinking to make gross judgments that a particular client-therapist engagement was a 'success' or a 'failure.' We can recognize that if the undertaking received the sincere efforts of both, some benefits almost certainly resulted, and we need to accept that those benefits were less than might be desired. Nevertheless, there is merit both in trying to approach that ideal more frequently and in accepting that we will always fall short of it."

Fisch: "I've Had My Full Share"

Richard Fisch, a professor of psychiatry at Stanford, has been a pioneer in research devoted to problem-solving therapy. Along with his colleagues at the Mental Research Institute in Palo Alto, Fisch has written extensively on issues related to reliable therapeutic intervention and assessing and maneuvering client positions. His best-known works include Change. Principles of Problem Formation and Problem Resolution (1974, with P. Watzlawick and J. Weakland) and The Tactics of Change: Doing Therapy Briefly (1982, with J. Weakland and L. Segal). Since Fisch believes that the therapist assumes much of the responsibility for treatment, he or she also shares most of the burden of success or failure, an outcome that can be easily measured: Either the client's problem is resolved or it is not. In Fisch's words:

"Like most therapists, I've had my full share of failures. Yet in thinking back over those cases, I can't recall anything particularly dramatic. In the course of my career I've been blessed, if an atheist can be allowed to use that word, with only one suicide. Looking back on that suicide, doing a lot of think ‑ ing about it after it happened , and discussing it with colleagues, I still could not see anything that should have been done differently. So even that tragic failure left me very puzzled.

"The great bulk of my failures have been more mundane — mostly patients dropping out of treatment when the problem hadn 't been resolved and there had been obvious dissatisfaction on their part, as well as mine, that things just had not gotten anywhere. On other occasions there have been more disturbing failures, disturbing because progress had occurred, but then, inexplicably, things started to break down.

"I think my experience with failures is a reflection of the way I see my work. I imagine this is probably the case with most therapists: How they view failure, what they view as failure, how they react to it, how they define their reactions, I t hink is likely to reflect the very framework they use in doing t herapy. For example, a therapist who operates with a model t hat emphasizes personal growth would likely see the outcome of failures as contributing to his or her personal growth.

" For me, therapy is what I'd call a challenging and com ‑ pelling chess game in which success and failure are fairly clearly demarcated. If I can help resolve the patient's complaint, that 's a success. If treatment has to end on an unresolved note, it's a failure. Happily, it's a friendly chess game in which it's either win-win or lose-lose. (And like any good chess-player/problem - solver, I always want to go for checkmate .)

"For that reason then, I don 't like to fail and, while I've tried becoming philosophical about failure, the truth of the matter is I don 't like it and I probably never will. I don 't try to soften the failure by explaining to myself or anybody else that, 'oh, it was an unmotivated patient or a too resistant patient,' t hat kind of thing. If you 're committed to a problem -solving ap ‑ proach, you find yourself looking for your own mistakes, accepting responsibility for the direction, course, and effectiveness of treatment.

"In a number of cases that have not worked out, I've

often felt quite puzzled. I've reviewed case notes, my recollec- t i ons of what I had said and done, and still found myself no more enlightened as to what I could have done differently. There are a number of instances, then, in which I can 't say I l earned anything and I had to shrug my shoulders and go on to t he next case and give it my best shot.

"There have been, however, many other times I've been able to learn from my mistakes. In reviewing those errors, very often I saw that I had intervened too quickly or with insufficient planning. Sometimes I overestimated the patient's willingness to take suggested action; I had not paid enough attention t o information indicating that he or she was still hesitant to accept some task or suggestion.

"Another mistake I've been able to learn from is getting i nto arguments with a patient. At the time I'm arguing I'm not aware of it; but where some cases have failed I can see that my best intentions of trying to get them to understand something was just arguing. You can usually tell when you 're arguing be - cause you 're talking too much. You can sense you 're working t oo hard.

"I think it's always important to pay careful attention to a patient's position or frame of reference. My failure to do that in one case shook me because I had misused my sense of humor. I'm accustomed to using humor in treatment. Sometimes it just falls flat, but often it can help. This is a case where I learned how important it is to pay attention to people 's positions, and my misplaced sense of humor brought that truth home to me.

"I was working with the parents of a young boy. He was about ten and had a congenital kidney condition which required his needing dialysis several times a week. His parents were com - ing in because he was socially withdrawn and having peer difficulties at school and in the neighborhood . His parents attributed his trouble to his medical condition and the unusual treatments he required. They believed that the boy, accordingly, felt inferior to other children, a bit like a freak, and they had been attempting, therefore, to make him feel normal. However, they went about it in such a studied way that they had created the reverse effect. They were unwittingly highlighting his medical condition, and I felt it important that they stop.

"Most of what they had been doing was to reassure him repeatedly that he was 'just like other kids.' But since this was obviously not the case, these 'reassurances' confirmed that he was so different it couldn 't even be acknowledged. I didn 't have much trouble convincing them to depart from that tack and instead take one in which they would accept the difficulties he was having and his difference from other kids more matter-of-factly. I remember that they felt relief since they could now relax and be more honest. They readily agreed to try that out in t he forthcoming week.

"When they returned the next session, they said they had t r ied the new strategy and had already seen signs of some bene - fit t o their child. I felt quite pleased with this outcome , but I made a serious error in the latter part of that session. They had been emphasizing how concerned they were for their child 's feelings—his feeling socially isolated, his feeling estranged from other children—and were now relieved to see some daylight at t he end of that tunnel. Focusing on their concern about how he was adjusting to other children, I attempted to reassure them by li ghtening the tone. I wanted to convey to them that 'while you 're very worried about your child and how he 's getting along, he will be doing okay, he 'll be getting on in school, get - ti ng along well with other kids, and you 'll find out that things will go okay for him .' Unfortunately I used an expression that people commonly use, that parents commonly use, about their children: 'Our kids grow up and we lose them .' I meant, of course, that we lose them in the sense that they lead their own i ndependent lives and are no longer dependent on the nuclear family.

"I had some misgivings as soon as the words left my mouth . Their faces darkened , and since it was the end of the session anyhow, they walked out stonily. We had set up an appointment for the next week but they didn 't show up, nor would they return my calls. So I had to speculate about what had happened. I believe that because of the sequence of events in that session, and the particular change occurring when I at - t empted to 'reassure' them in the way I did, it undermined an improving picture. While it was true that they wanted him to have a happy adjustment to other children, their concern re-

fleeted a deeper fear—that his life would be a shorter one because of his medical condition and therefore they wanted him t o
be as happy as he could be for the time he did remain on this earth.
I neglected to pay attention to that more fundamental fear and
blithely addressed my comments to their current con ‐ cern about
his adjustment. Unfortunately , I used wording that must have
seemed callous to them since they refused to come back or to
answer any of my calls.

"That case, among all my cases, shook me up the most.
Things had been going rather well, and yet because of a misplaced use of lightness, it ended quite dismally. Nevertheless, I
was able to learn from that experience—to pay attention to peo ‐
ple 's sensibilities, values, and frames of reference, not to take
t hose things for granted, and to carefully match my phrasing
t o people 's 'positions.' It doesn 't mean that I have not made
similar errors since—I have—but I think less so than I would
have done if I had not had this rather dramatic failure.

"In summary, then, I've been able, at least on occasion, t o
profit from failures by being able to identify mistakes that I made
in a case or in a session, so that I will be in a better posi‐ t i on
not to make those same mistakes in the future. It 's not really
dissimilar from any other craft."

Ellis: "At Least Three Errors"

Albert Ellis has been motivated by achievement and pro ‐
ductivity for the past four decades. Surely one of the most pro ‐
lific writers in the field, he has published hundreds of papers
and   books,   established training centers on behalf of
rationalemotive therapy (RET), and traveled around the world
present‐ ing workshops on the efficacy of his techniques. While
his the ‐ ory was still in its formative stage, Ellis experienced failure
with one of his first cases with the experimental methodology
that evolved into cognitive therapy.

He recalls his work with Jeff, a young man who had been
seriously depressed. Although the client responded quite well to
active-directive therapy and recovered for a number of years, he
eventually returned to treatment with symptoms as severe as

ever. Ellis countered Jeff 's relapse by vigorously disputing his irrational beliefs and using a variety of behavioral imagery and RET interventions. Ellis continues the story:

"To no avail. Jeff occasionally managed to lift his depression, but as soon as business slowed down he reverted to severe self-downing and despair. After twenty -three sessions of RET his wife insisted that something deeper than his dire need for success must be troubling him. She was very angry at me for not helping him, and forced him to go for psychoanalysis. Eight months later he attempted suicide and had to be hospitalized for several weeks. Since that time he has maintained a marginal existence. He would like to return to RET, as he remembers his original success with it, but his wife will not allow this and mainly keeps him on antidepressants, which seem to help mod - erately.

"This case made a notable impression on me because in t hinking about it, I concluded that I had made at least three kinds of errors:

1.   I had diagnosed Jeff as a severe depressive but not as being endogenously depressed. I know that his father also had bouts of depression but failed to investigate his other close relatives. I now think that endogenous depression probably runs in the family.

2.   While seeing Jeff for the second time I failed to urge him strongly enough to try antidepressant medication con - comitant with the psychotherapy . I misled myself by re- membering the good results we had obtained without medi- cation. I now believe that Jeff could have profited most from psychotherapy and pharmacotherapy combined .

3. I failed to urge Jeff to bring his wife fully into the therapy process and only had one session with her. Instead I prob - ably should have arranged continuing sessions with her and with both of them .

"As a result of my failing with Jeff and with several simi- lar cases of severe depression, I now take greater care to look for evidence of endogenous depression, to enlist other family

members in the therapeutic process, and to ferret out and ac‐
tively dispute —and teach my clients to dispute —their dogmatic
shoulds, oughts, and musts ."

Lazarus: "I Blamed Myself Entirely"

Arnold A. Lazarus, the founder of multimodel therapy, is
a consummate pragmatist who has struggled to integrate all as‐
pects of the person (biological, affective, cognitive, behavioral,
imaginal, sensory, and interpersonal) into a unified process of
psychological assessment and treatment. Usually fluent and elo‐
quent in spontaneous discourse, Lazarus experienced frustra‐
t i on, puzzlement, and blockage when he attempted to record
his ideas on failure. Eventually, he was able to overcome some
of his resistance to the subject by focusing on his evolution as a
t herapist. In his words:

"I was thinking back to the way I used to feel in the early
days of my clinical practice when I failed and how I feel today,
and I think the difference is that initially it used to bother me
t r emendously. I suppose I blamed myself entirely, wondered
whether I was cut out to be a therapist at all, and felt horrible.
I think what happens as you gain more experience and more
success is that you get a better balanced view of situations and
can take your failures in stride. You come to realize that the
state of the science and the art is such that you are not going to
win them all. As I like to tell my students, I don 't think that
t herapists should feel, using a football analogy, that they must
t ake every patient into the end zone. You start with somebody
at the twenty- or thirty-yard line and if you can advance them
t o midfield and pass to somebody else who can go still further,
t hat 's terrific and that 's not failure."

After wrestling with the thorny issue of defining what
exactly constitutes a failure in his view, Lazarus demonstrated
how with decades of experience he has been able to accept him ‐
self as less than perfect. Instead of condemning himself as he
once did, he has tried to adopt an attitude of self-acceptance,
self-inquiry, and forgiveness just as he feels toward his clients.
Yet, when he confronts a case beyond his power to cure, Laz‐
arus, like Ellis, cannot help but feel hooked:

"I have a patient I'm failing with at the moment who puzzles the hell out of me. She is a bright, attractive, vivacious, intelligent, well-educated woman who is doing extremely well in her work, drives a Porsche, and dresses in expensive clothes but has this kind of "fear, fear, fear" as she calls it. There is an ob - vious obsessive component to her makeup in which the fear that she might be fearful is predominant. I tell you I have tried every- t hing in my arsenal, and I have not made a dent. I think I'm t herapist number six who has failed to have an impact. The only t hing that seems to help her are medications from time to time, but there is a rampant, almost malignant, obsessive-compulsive quality that is impossible thus far to really do much about, and I feel very, very frustrated. I feel sorry for her. I would like to be able to do something to mitigate her misery. She is entitled t o a happier trip on this crazy globe of ours."

When confronted with painfully unsuccessful cases such as this, Lazarus works hard on himself by repeating thoughts he might confide to his students or clients:

"I don 't expect to succeed all of the time. By succeed I mean really score touchdowns. I expect to be helpful, facilita- tive, useful, significant to the majority of the people who con - sult me, and I think I am. But when I'm not, I guess I'm in- clined to view it as, well, it's the imperfect state of the art and science. I did my best and what can I tell you ? Sometimes I t hink my failures are due to the fact that certain people are so fixed upon maintaining their status quo that neither you, nor I, nor a plutonium bomb would budge them ."

Corey: "I Do Struggle at Times"

Gerald Corey is one of the premier textbook writers in the field today, best regarded for his student-centered approach to t r aining therapists. He has ten books currently in print on a wide range of subjects including group work , ethics, theories of t herapy, personal growth , and professional issues. From high atop a mountain in Southern California, Corey is a virtual fac- t ory of professional productivity, churning out successive edi- t i ons of his best-selling books. Most recently published are the fourth editions of I Never Knew I Had a Choice (in press, with

Marianne Schneider Corey) and **Theory and Practice o f Coun -
seling and Psychotherapy** (in press). In his words:

"I would like to share an experience when I was co-lead-
ing a training group. A woman asked me at one point what I
t hought of her and whether I liked her or not. Since she was
one of my former students, she was particularly interested in
how I viewed her and how she measured up in my eyes. Before
I could answer, my co-leader intervened by saying, 'Before Jerry
responds, would you be willing to tell him why it's important
for you to know how he views you or what he thinks of you ? '
She thought for a moment and responded , 'Well, I respect you
and like you, yet sometimes I think that I'm insignificant in
your eyes and that you think I'm weird .'

"For some reason, I did not respond to her. During the
break my co-leader asked me, "What was going on with you?
How come you didn 't answer it? Was there any particular reason ? ' I told my co-leader that I felt put on the spot, that I felt
uncomfortable, that I didn 't know what to say. My co-leader re-
t orted with, 'Damn it, that 's exactly what you should have said!
That 's what we teach the participants to do —to give their here-
and-now reactions.' My co-leader also recognized that she was
not following her inclination to keep pressing and find out why
I was not responding. She assumed that I had a reason for my
lack of response, yet she didn 't check it out immediately.

"Other participants in the group also noticed my unwillingness to respond to this person, and they too assumed that I
had my reasons. Several members began to talk about this incident in a subsequent group session and they expressed their
reactions to me. They too wanted to know why I had remained
so quiet. Some of them thought that I was using a technique,
while others got angry and told me they thought I was insensitive toward her.

"I then told the group and this woman that I was not
using a technique, nor was there a reason for my failure to respond to her, except that I felt put on the spot and was somewhat at a loss for words. I let the group know that I do struggle
at times with giving my immediate here-and-now reactions when
I am confronted , and that I become evasive or sometimes say

nothing at all. I acknowledged that I had made a mistake. She did deserve a response from me, and 1 regretted holding back my perceptions. Initially, this woman did put me on the spot with her question. However, my co-leader skillfully put the spotlight back on her by asking her to state her reasons for wanting to know how I viewed her. This former student took a chance in letting me know how she felt about me, and certainly some response other than a blank screen was appropriate. Even if I had merely told her of my immediate reaction when expectations are put upon me, 1 could at least have said this.

"It was interesting to both my co-leader and me that group members often discount their appropriate reactions, such as annoyance with a leader's behavior, by finding a justification for that behavior. They were quite willing to give away their power rather than stick by their own convictions. They had a difficult time accepting that a group leader, especially one they li ked and respected, could make a mistake.

"I again very humbly recognize that it isn't easy to do what one knows is appropriate, and that under pressure we sometimes revert to old patterns of behavior. In my eyes, alt hough I did make a mistake, the situation did not turn into a failure because I was willing to explore what happened with my co-leader and the group members. Had I been unwilling to accept that I had behaved inappropriately, then I would indeed have failed. In this particular case, all of us learned something from my mistake ."

Moustakas: "I Felt a Deep Distress"

Clark Moustakas is one of the founders and chief propo nents of the humanistic psychology movement, having estab li shed a graduate institute and written numerous books on the subject. Most notable are his books on loneliness and existential therapy with children. Unlike other contributors who submitted tapes or written accounts, Moustakas preferred to be i nterviewed on the subject:

"Rather than focusing on fears of failure or failure as such, which do not connect with my experience as a therapist,

I prefer to concentrate on dimensions or aspects of the therapy process in which I have experienced doubt or inadequacy, in which I have felt that I failed to reach the person.

"Early on as a therapist, I had been educated and trained in nondirective therapy. Soon after graduation,   I worked with a client who had problems with women and wanted my advice, my suggestions, for solution of this problem . I effectively em – ployed the methodology in which I had been trained —that is, I l i s tened carefully, I reflected thoughts, feelings, and content ac– curately. I accepted his statements and shared his concerns. I was criticized by this client. He reprimanded me, saying that I was just repeating his words, just paraphrasing his expressions. I believed I had added a twist of my own, but it did not register with him. He became angry with me. 'You are not telling me what to do. I want your advice.'   I responded that what he wanted was not compatible with my way of helping people. I believed that if he continued to explore the problem , a solution would emerge. He said with apparent calm, 'You remind me of a former girlfriend. Talking to her was like throwing a wet sponge against a blank wall!' The client terminated the session early, saying it was a waste of his time. He did not return ."

Moustakas does not, however, view this case as a failure. He was employing his method of training effectively. It was sim– ply the wrong model for this client. He had not, as yet, begun t o question his training and was adhering to what he had been t aught. In reflecting on the example, he indicated that this ex – perience opened an entirely new realm of questioning his educa– t i on and reexamining his strict adherence to the techniques he had learned. It opened the door to experimenting with his own presence as a way of facilitating change and growth.

"If I saw this man today, I would be more interactive, more confrontive; still I would not give him advice, but I prob – ably would be more directive, more interpretive, and more self-disclosing. My interactions with him were on an 'I—It' basis; I feel certain that faced with a similar situation today, I would be more responsive as a self, entering into an 'I -Thou ' relationship ."

Another problem that Moustakas noted in himself has to do with the setting of limits. "In the early years ," he confesses, "my timing was often off ." He explains:

"Over a period of thirty-five years, I have met many trou -bled children in therapy, enraged and destructive children. In t he early years, I would not know how or when to set a limit. I would resist setting limits and would put myself in a situation of anxiety. I would sense that the child was moving toward a destructive act but I would not move to intervene. Then I would sometimes be physically attacked . I would lose ground in the t herapeutic process and would feel that I was starting all over again with the child. The child would become increasingly en-raged in my permissive world, and would get out of control. Sometimes I would become angry, too , more at myself for wait-ing too long ."

Moustakas notes much improvement in his limit-setting skills. He relates a recent incident that occurred while he was on an airplane. A young child of three or four was seated behind him and began kicking the back of his seat. He turned and gave her a look that said, "I don 't like what you are doing ." She con -t i nued to kick. He then turned around again and put his feelings i nto words: " I don 't like what you are doing. I am very upset t hat you are kicking my seat. I am not able to do my work. Please stop ." For the remainder of the journey the child did not kick the seat. As he left the airplane, Moustakas spoke to her again: " I want to thank you . You helped make this a pleasant t r ip for me by not kicking the seat." The child replied, "Thank you ." Moustakas says that in earlier years he would not have set this limit but would have suffered throughout the trip and perhaps become irritated and resentful.

Moustakas's feelings of self-doubt and inadequacy were sparked by another case with a child. A thirteen-year-old had mentioned how poorly he was feeling physically, how no one cared about him, how other kids made fun of his peculiarities, how his parents constantly criticized him. He did not think t here was any solution. Every day brought headaches, dizziness, and sickness. No one listened to this boy. He felt that each day brought nothing but misery into his life.

Moustakas had experienced painful tensions in being with this client, struggling to decide how to intervene and wondering if t he client should be hospitalized. He continued to work with this boy, listening carefully, reflecting what he heard, and feeling concerned and caring. During the third session, the boy be — gan to reveal creative resources for dealing with his family, the school, and himself. He began to explore ways to meet the crisis. He began to disclose an inward power that would show others what he could do, especially in art and science activities.

The director of psychological services pulled the file on t his client and set up a special meeting with the consulting psychiatrist and staff of the facility. Moustakas was told the meeting was mandatory but not that his client was to be its focus. When he arrived, the consulting psychiatrist inquired if everyone present knew the purpose of the meeting. Moustakas replied that he did not. The psychiatrist was distressed that he had not been informed. The staff reviewed the first two sessions and agreed that the youth needed a more controlled intervent i on than Moustakas was providing. They had not read the notes of the third session because Moustakas had not yet placed them in the file. When he reported on the dramatic change in the client, the staff still agreed that hospitalization was needed. They did not value his work with this client. They were disdainful of his conviction that the client held the light, resources, and determination to direct the course of his life and was finally beginning to face his problems. He just needed time and support. In a surprising shift of perspective, the consulting psychiatrist supported Moustakas, and the case was left to his management. Moustakas experienced pain at the lack of support from his colleagues, but he knew that, due to their different orientations, t hey did not understand or value his way of working with children.

Moustakas believes that the mistakes that therapists make occur because they persist in employing a methodology or tech — nique that is not useful—one that is not helpful to the client and is not responsive to the client's own therapeutic sensitivities. There is also a problem of going too far in having a client be responsible for everything, especially with children who might not be developmental^ ready for what a therapist is requiring. He offered an example of a student intern he was observing in play t herapy. A young child had come into the playroom looking very frightened. She walked to the middle of the playroom , sucking her thumb , remaining speechless. The therapist too was silent. The child began to cry and finally asserted, " I want to leave." The therapist told her, "I hear that you want to leave, but we have forty-five minutes left here ."

The child continued to cry and insisted on leaving. Her voice became less assertive, more begging, more strained. The t herapist continued to say, " 1 hear that you want to leave, but we have thirty-five minutes left and you need to decide what you want to do here ." Then, a few minutes later, " I know you want to leave but we have thirty more minutes. You 're wasting time. What do you want to do ? "

At one point the child looked down at her shoes and, no - ti cing that they were untied , asked the therapist to tie them for her. He told her that in the playroom "children do things for themselves. You 'll have to tie them yourself." " But," she whis- pered, "I don 't know how ." He replied, " 1 hear that you don 't know how, but you 'll need to decide what you want to do about that ."

In talking with Moustakas later, the student was embar- rassed and filled with shame. Confessing that he simply did not know what to do, he believed he was following a key premise of t herapy —namely, that the client must be responsible for what occurs in the session. He knew that something was wrong but held onto this principle rather than responding to what the im- mediate moment required.

Another challenge facing Moustakas as a therapist in his work with adolescents arose when the personality or relation- ship problem was resolved but an underlying character disorder remained. The disorder, Moustakas believes, ultimately created a strength in the adolescent that was used destructively. But Moustakas seldom addressed this problem since it was not part of the therapy contract. "I feel that at times I have surrendered i mportant life values in remaining tied to a client's goals in ther- apy. I have failed to address the moral and ethical issues with many of these clients."

Two examples came to mind. One involved an adolescent who cheated an insurance company and excitedly told Mous- t akas of his success. The client felt good, strong, powerful. Al-

t hough this boy 's self-esteem had improved in therapy and his
personal resources had been strengthened, he was using them for
purposes that were unethical. Moustakas did not address this issue
with the adolescent. He listened but let the matter stand j ust as
presented.

Another example had to do with a thirteen-year-old boy
who had been bullied and teased at school. Through his therapy
he began to gain self-esteem and inner strength. In one session
he reported , with pride, that he had beaten up a peer and
t hrown him down a flight of stairs. The client took great pleasure in describing the serious injuries he had inflicted on a boy
who once had beaten him on the school playground. Moustakas
confronted this client with his use of power to defeat and hurt
others: "

"I felt a deep distress that I had helped him discover resources for self-assertiveness and use of personal power and that
he was using those strengths to attack and injure others, that he
was pleased and even bragging and gloating at his successes. We
grappled with these issues for awhile and he became increasingly
angry with me. He didn 't want to hear my opinions or judg -
ments, but I continued to express my sense of wrongness in
how he was using his strength. Sneeringly, he told me I did not
understand the ethics of teenage life or society. He terminated
t he therapy with the support of his parents, who were pleased
with his new strength and ability to conquer others in his everyday world ."

Moustakas continues to be concerned about the implica-
t i ons of how people in therapy apply what they learn to the
practical challenges of relationships and life. Evident through -
out the Moustakas interview is a concept of helping that mini-
mizes judgments of success or failure. Emphasis is placed on
being with the client as part of a continuing process of
natural
unfolding.

Emerging Themes

There seems to be a consensus among this sample of
prominent therapists that failure is not the same as a strategy
t hat does not work. While each voice expressed the concept in a

highly individualized way, the chorus sings out a single message: Failure, as such, is not a useful word to describe what happens when things do not work out as expected .

Bugental sees himself as failing the client when he does not provide the environment in which the client can make significant life changes. This shortcoming may stem from a lack of i nvestment or presence, an unwillingness to confront and challenge the client, or even one 's own neurotic lapses. While Bugental believes he sometimes fails his clients because it is his responsibility to help them change, he never sees himself as a failure. He cautions us not to generalize our judgments of therapy but to view each therapist/client interaction as containing elements of success and failure.

For Fisch and Ellis, whether or not a patient's problem is resolved is the chief indicator of success or failure. Underlying t he determination of failure is the theoretical model espoused and the definition of success inherent in that framework.

Moustakas says that treatment suffers when the therapist is too closely bound to a model and gives this as a reason why one client left him. He emphasizes the relationship between t herapist and client as the most critical factor in therapeutic effectiveness. Although he acknowledges having difficulty setting limits with children in treatment, "failure" is not a term he would use to describe this impediment. Rather, he would say t hat the connection between him and the child was not yet strong enough and that limit setting was but one factor in a multi-faceted relationship.

Lazarus sets realistic goals for himself, expecting to be helpful to the majority of people who consult him, yet knowing this will not happen with everyone. He is especially articulate in describing the incredible frustration that comes from wanting desperately to help somebody but not knowing what else to do. The idea of helping clients make progress along some dimen - sion, any dimension, removes the need to make an all-or-nothing j udgment regarding success or failure.

Corey believes failure occurs when therapists are not willing to explore and take responsibility for their contribution to t he problem . He describes the familiar feeling of being frozen with inaction—knowing that some intervention is called for, but j ust not knowing what to do. Particularly in group settings, where every therapist's action is magnified a dozen times, such passivity can be devastating in its effects. His story depicts how, because of the stature and power ascribed to us as therapists, clients often make incredible allowances in overlooking our errors. Even when we are blatantly off target in some interven- t i on, clients tend to excuse our behavior. Thus we are often al- lowed to escape failure without detection , even when we know, all too well, we have made a mistake.

Ellis demonstrates the kind of analytic self-scrutiny that promotes a vivid autopsy of failed cases. He reviews his con - duct, what he did, and the results and frankly concludes he missed a crucial organic factor operating in the client's symptom - atology and also alienated the wife of his client. In his opin - ion, failures are simply opportunities for reflection and further learning. This open and honest attitude enables him to learn from his mistakes and to study the process by which therapy goes awry.

Therapists are seen by each contributor as human and fallible, guilty, at times, of their own neurotic lapses, of mis- reading what clients present, utilizing inappropriate techniques, or not attending to the client's frame of reference. All of these reports reflect a discomfort when things go wrong, a willing- ness to examine the faulty situation and discover the therapist's part in it, a commitment to use what is learned, and an ability t o move on.

Fisch views treatment as a sort of friendly chess game in which success depends on whether the client won or lost (even if it cannot be determined how the match proceeded). He has developed a willingness to accept full responsibility for negative results along with a forgiving nature that allows him to shrug off disappointment and move on to the next challenge.

Lazarus cautions us not to expect to score touchdowns but rather to have a balanced view of therapy with realistic ex - pectations that will allow us to take failure in stride. Bugental echoes this notion in urging therapists to strive for the ideal more often while acknowledging, at the same time, that we will always fall short of it.

All these reports also acknowledge the client's contribu - t i on in determining the success of therapy. Both Bill and Nina engaged Bugental's services and determined how long and how effectively they would work with him; Fisch 's couple angrily departed following his insensitive remark; Lazarus was therapist number six with his troublesome client; Jeff, in listening to his wife rather than Ellis, sought treatment with another clinician; Corey was brought to task by a group member; Moustakas's early client failed to get what he wanted and left.

Each of these prominent therapists may conceptualize his failures a bit differently, just as they are all somewhat unified in t heir belief that refinements in technique and theory occur as much from their mistakes as from their triumphs. They all share a respect for their failures, and hence are utterly frank with themselves in admitting their part in negative outcomes. Such self-honesty and internal clarity are prerequisites for a serious analysis of therapists' flaws and imperfections.

8

What Goes Wrong:
Common Themes

The title of this chapter presumes that it is possible to identify the exact circumstances, factors, and behavior that lead to failure in therapy. And we will indeed attempt to do just that. From an examination of relevant literature and information gleaned from therapists discussing their experiences of failure in therapy, however, we recognize that a good part of the time, perhaps even in a majority of cases, the specific reason given for less than satisfying results rarely presents the full picture. Although we may offer elaborate theories or hypotheses to explain our failures, we rarely discover the whole truth.

There are many reasons why it is so difficult to deduce the causes of failure. For one, when things go wrong, clients are unlikely to tell us the real reasons they left treatment. Months later it may filter back to us through another source that the client did not approve of our style of dress or the way we addressed him or something we said that seemed heartless. Secondly, clients often do not **know** why they felt unhappy with the way things were proceeding. Thirdly, our own suspicions of what went wrong are clouded by our need to appear in a favorable light, to deny mistakes and poor judgment, to avoid responsibility for negative results. Lastly, the therapeutic encounter, with all its nuances and intricacies, is probably far too complex for us ever to ascertain a single reason for failure. More than likely, a combination of factors are operating.

In this spirit of caution regarding simplistic explanations for failure, we present those variables that, either singly or in combination, are most often the culprits. They can be divided into factors attributed to the client, those that are the result of

t he therapist's behavior, variables that stem from interactive effects in the therapy process (such as the examples in Chapter
Six), and influences outside the therapy that sabotage results.
Since the focus of this book is the therapist's experience of
fail- ure, we emphasize the variables that directly emerge from
the t herapist's deficiencies.

Clients Destined to Fail

In many cases, clients are lost because of what we do or
what we fail to do. Yet in other cases, regardless of what we do
or say, no matter how careful we may be, how sensitive, skilled,
or helpful, there are some clients who are determined to avoid
i mprovement. Whether because of an unconscious tendency to
sabotage progress or a deliberate effort to circumvent the most
diligent clinician, certain people will probably never succeed in
therapy. In the previous chapter, Lazarus described just such a
client. Even though he used all the resources available to him,
Lazarus found that the client still seemed miserable. There
are certain personality or mood disorders, certain defense
mechanisms, certain people who are sufficiently impaired in
t heir judgment, in their capacity for insight, that they are un -
likely ever to change much. For such people, progress in treatment is not measured in weeks, but rather in decades.

People who abruptly end their therapy before work has
been completed have been found to have certain qualities. They are
most likely to be a member of a minority group, to be young
adults, to have insurance coverage with maximum bene - fits, and
to have been referred by another professional within a clinic
facility. They are also likely to have situational, acute, or
adjustment reactions that they blame on external factors out of t
heir control (Greenspan and Kulish, 1985).

In a review of cases of failure in psychoanalytic treatment, Colson, Lewis, and Horwitz (1985) found that clients
doomed to fail had certain characteristics in common . It is perhaps familiar to most practitioners that chronicity of symptoms
and degree of disturbance represent the standard predictors of a
poor prognosis. Additionally, clients with problems of impulse

control, clients who lack support systems, those who are older, who lack a sense of humor, who are impatient, who tend to ex − t ernalize and lack psychological sophistication, are less likely to i mprove in therapy (Stone, 1985).

Those who work with seductive personalities commonly encounter great difficulty with clients exhibiting borderline qualities. Based on a personal sample of fifty-one borderline clients, Stone (1985), an expert who has devoted his life to specializing with this group, reports a 4 0 percent failure rate! If an **expert** on this condition can help only half of his clients, one wonders how those therapists who meet just a few borderline cases could ever hope to avoid failure much of the time.

It is not that we ought to feel pessimistic whenever we are faced with clients who have poor prognoses in the literature − on the contrary, such a hopeless attitude would likely contrib − ute to a self-fulfilling prophecy. Yet, while maintaining an optimistic attitude , it is also sensible to be realistic about what is within our power to change. Indeed the therapists in the pre − ceding chapter universally agreed that, despite their best efforts, t herapy sometimes fails. Kouw (personal communication , 1988) reminds us that the patient's suitability for psychotherapy should not be taken for granted any more than that of the therapist. Much of the success of treatment depends on the client's motivation, personality, and attitude. We would do well to remind ourselves that a client's failure is not necessarily our own. With this in mind, we need no longer fear high-risk cases.

In a satirical article on the therapist's fear of failure and reluctance to take high-risk cases, Menaham (1986) describes strategies for treating dead clients. He quite rightly points out t here is a paucity of literature on the subject and that, in general, most clinicians shy away from doing therapy with the dead because of the high failure rate. Dead clients are **very** resistant, prone to silence, passivity, flattened affect, and a pungent odor. Furthermore, they rarely pay their bills. Indeed, there are cer− t ain people who are about as responsive to therapeutic treat− ment as the deceased. They may be those who exhibit certain personality disorders or psychotic processes. They may be those who are too well defended or have been wounded by an incom −

petent helper earlier in life. As comforting as this information might be —that there are some people nobody could help —most t herapy failures stem from other sources.

When the Therapist Fails

From her analysis of treatm ent failures in family therapy, Coleman (1 9 8 5) found the following factors to have been most prevalent:

- Failure to understand the real nature of the presenting prob − lem including the circumstances surrounding the referral
- Insufficient alliance with family members or a weak thera− peutic relationship with the client
- Theoretical omissions or inconsistent interventions
- Waning energy' or professional transition

On a more universal scale, extrapolating from her sample, Cole− man concludes that failures had less to do with conscious or un − conscious wrongdoing than with therapists having been surprised by "unforeseen entanglements."

Operating with an individual psychodynamic treatment model, H. S. Strean has found that failures most often occur when the therapist is poorly motivated because of negative feel− ings toward the client. He cites as an example a case in which, even after two years of treatment, the client, Albert, a philos− ophy professor, became considerably more impaired. The rela− t i onship began in the initial interview with an interrogation by t he belligerent client concerning Strean 's credentials:

> Usually after a first interview, I feel an eager and
> i nterested anticipation of the next session, much
> li ke the feeling of getting ready to go on a journey.
> This time, however, I found myself obsessing about
> Albert after he left. I knew from my analytic train −
> ing that obsessing is a sign of mixed feelings.
>
> After my first interview with Albert, and
> after a number of succeeding sessions, I engaged in

fantasied arguments in which I was trying to ward off a bully who made me feel weak and vulnerable. Obviously, Albert threatened me, and it was difficult for me to acknowledge this truth , so I argued with him in fantasy. In hindsight, I have to admit my work with him was a failure in that I could not give him the help he was entitled to receive and was, I believe, capable of using   [Strean and Freeman, 1988, pp. 186 -1 8 7],

With remarkable candor Strean reviewed his conduct during the sessions and concluded he had made a number of significant mistakes—all triggered by his negative attitude toward the client. We summarize the range of errors as an example of the valuable case analysis that is possible after failures:

- He lost his objectivity and let himself be pulled into the client 's manipulative ploys.
- Because of feelings of threat, jealousy, and competition , he perpetuated a continual power struggle.
- He often made the "correct" interpretation or said the "right" words, but in a tone of voice that was more hostile t han empathic.
- He spent much of the time trying to prove to the client (flashbacks to his father) that he knew what he was doing.
- Although he was aware his counter-transference feelings were getting in the way, he could not monitor or confront them sufficiently, nor did he seek supervision or therapy to resolve them .
- He retreated behind the mask of cold, objective analyst in order to be punitive rather than adopting a posture of em pathy and support.

Strean concludes his self-analysis: "Actually my work with him should not really be called psychoanalytic treatment. It was more of an interpersonal struggle between two men who felt un comfortable with each other, each one trying to prove his po t ency to the other and to himself" (p. 191).

Moving to the other end of the theoretical spectrum , Foa and Emmelkamp (1983) examined failures in a behavior therapy context. Consistent with this model in which the therapist accepts the bulk of responsibility for treatment outcomes, the authors found miscalculations and misdiagnoses to be the greatest problem . They cite as examples several diagnostic errors in which the therapist failed to identify variables in the client's environment that continued to maintain dysfunctional symptoms. They describe another instance of misjudgment in which a therapist attempted to treat suspected psychogenic chronic pain that, in fact, turned out to be caused by undiagnosed cancer. They also mention failures caused by not properly following through on treatment plans that would have worked , as well as failing to help the client generalize new insights or learned responses to situations in the real world.

It would seem that much of the time failures in therapy can be prevented if those due to the therapist's behavior or client/therapist interaction are detected early enough by the therapist's honest self-analysis or, better yet, by seeking consultation in supervision or personal therapy. Yet, it should be noted , even with the most diligent practitioners, seeking the best possible supervision, things between a particular client and therapist may just not work out because of their interpersonal chemistry. Nevertheless, the frequency of process failures, and those due to bungled therapeutic skills and counter-transference issues, can be significantly reduced through systematic self-study.

When the Process Fails

In a review of determinants for the premature interruption of therapy, Levinson, McMurray, Podell, and Weiner (1 9 7 8) discovered that 87 percent of dropouts were caused by factors relative to the therapy process. That is, more than internal factors such as the client's poor motivation or negative attitude , or outside influences such as family interference, the majority of failures were the direct result of the therapy process or the therapist's behavior. In other words, it is some variable within the therapist's control, or some aspect of his or her performance, t hat most often leads to failure. Despite our collective fantasy t hat when clients drop out or feel dissatisfied with progress it is t heir own fault, it would appear, at least from this study, that t he therapist shares a large part of the responsibility. This idea was confirmed by the therapists who discussed their cases in the preceding chapter.   Bugental, for example, questioned the na- t ure of his investment with Bill; Moustakas acknowledged his difficulty setting limits and its impact on the children with whom he worked; and Fisch took responsibility for his mis- placed humor and the subsequent loss of his client.

It seems as if placing blame on the client's motivation , re- sistance, or defenses may be more of a weak excuse on the part of the therapist than a genuine reflection of reality. But then , in many of our cases, we have known this all along. At times it sounds utterly feeble to explain away a mistake or disaster as t he fault of some extraneous influence not in our control. When Bill Cosby was caught red-handed as a child standing in the mid - dle of the broken bed he had been bouncing on, he convincingly explained to his angry father that he did not do it—no matter how things looked. When his father demanded further elabora- ti on, Cosby claimed that while he was sleeping peacefully, a rob- ber sneaked in through the window and then jumped on the bed, breaking it with his weight, before slipping back out through t he window —leaving this poor innocent boy to take the rap. Cosby 's father paused a moment and then in a quiet voice re- minded him that there was no window in the room from which a robber could have entered. Without skipping a beat, Cosby re- plied: "Yeah, Dad, he took it with him ."

Most common among the causes of process failure are un - resolved transference experiences or dependency issues in the t herapeutic relationship (Herron and Rouslin, 1984). In these cases, separation conflicts are mismanaged or prematurely ter- minated.   Herron and Rouslin describe the scenario when the t herapist's own emotional attachment to a client becomes a form of symbiotic interdependence that is not easily broken. The therapist's unresolved issues of separation /individuation and parent/child bonding become mixed into the client's am - bivalence regarding the wish for continued intimacy versus free-

dom . When therapists feel threatened by these factors, they terminate treatment prematurely ; when they wish to guard against t
he sense of loss and inevitable mourning that accompanies
separation, they needlessly prolong the therapy while sacrificing t
he client's need for autonomy.

In the first case, failure occurs when the client's feelings
of abandonment lead to regression, isolation, rejection, loneliness, bitterness, or debilitating anxiety. An absolutely spectacular "cure " can quite easily be undone by the impatient, bored,
or insensitive therapist who might unduly rush treatment to its
unnatural conclusion. Perhaps by taking at face value the client
who says he feels much better, or maybe just to open a slot in
an overburdened schedule, the treatment is ended prematurely.
Partly to punish the heartless "parent/therapist," partly because
he lacks confidence and experience, the client may end up
worse than before he arrived. Not only is there a recurrence of
symptoms, but now there are newfound feelings of rage and
betrayal as well.

In the second variation, failure occurs when the client be −
comes so dependent on the therapist that the possibility of an
autonomous existence is even more remote. In an extreme ex −
ample of this type of disaster, a therapist abruptly decided to
stop working with a client who had become increasingly demanding and needy after having been taught by her therapist to
feel very grateful. This woman , who had been attending twice-
weekly sessions religiously for years, now found she could not
function at all when her therapist left town for even a week 's
vacation. (The therapist never took more than a week off at a
t i me since many of his clients felt this way.) Through the observations of a respected colleague, the therapist agreed it was time
t o wean this client from her dependence. (He also felt the ses−
sions had become tedious.) Even though for years it appeared as
if this client had made substantial gains in a number of areas, it
quickly became apparent when termination was discussed that
progress was more for the therapist's approval than for the client 's own good. Many failures result from the therapist's ignorance regarding the extent of the client's dependence or reluc−
t ance to confront this symbiotic intimacy and resolve it.

Another issue that often leads to problems relates to the t herapist's energy level. One such lapse is especially common among experienced therapists who, through years of practice, have developed an attitude that nothing much new ever occurs. They believe that most new clients present situations that are simply variations of a few basic themes presented over and over again. A client becomes angry toward the therapist and we im – mediately assume "transference reaction ." Another exhibits shyness and we assume "poor self-esteem and a fear of rejec- t i on ." These assumptions come from vast experience with hun – dreds of cases that seem to show consistent patterns. But to a certain extent we become jaded. We tend to see what we have seen innumerable times instead of what is really there. And be- fore long we may find ourselves failing to treat each case as unique and each client with a distinctly different history, per- sonality, and way of viewing the world even if the symptoms ap- pear familiar. What we gain in wisdom , we may lose in the fresh- ness and thorough way in which beginning clinicians treat each case as if nothing like it has ever occurred before.

While the beginner may fail through ignorance, the expe- rienced therapist may do so through neglect or a laissez-faire attitude. A good example of what can result from this perspec- tive of "I've seen it all before " is illustrated by the story of one t herapist. He felt regretful and appropriately censured by mem – bers of a group he was leading when he failed to gather suffi- cient background before intervening in a minimal way. He had been approached by a particularly shy and passive client who felt unable to speak up in the group. She solicited his help and support, which he interpreted to mean the need for gentle prod – ding during sessions. Since this was a relatively routine concern, he neglected to explore what personal meaning this inhibition held for the woman. In every group he led there had always been a shy person who needed drawing out. Assuming this was more of the same, he was startled at the horrible outcome of what he thought was a mild and innocent gesture.

He wished to nudge the client a bit by slipping her a note t hat read "force yourself to open your m outh ." The client's face became ashen and she trembled noticeably, although he had by then turned his attention to someone else who held the group 's focus. It was not until the next group meeting that the client had pulled herself together sufficiently to express her outrage—a reaction that positively shocked her well-meaning therapist. A victim of incest at age six, the client was often forced by her father to "open her m outh " to satisfy his lust. If she refused to open her mouth she had to take him in her anus instead. The unfortunate wording of the note, commanding her to force herself to open her mouth , naturally brought back a host of painful memories. While the therapist could perhaps be excused for inadvertently evoking this tragic material, he succeeded in alienating the incest victim and several group mem bers who thought he should have been better informed before he pushed somebody too far too fast.

As is the case with many therapeutic failures, the processing of the event, in retrospect, proved immediately beneficial. After the therapist acknowledged his error and worked things out with the client such that she felt much relieved to "open her m outh " in this context, attention moved to conflicts with t he leader in his role as authority and transference object. It was only in the quiet hours after the group disbanded that the therapist was able to scrutinize his defensiveness and examine his need to appear in control when caught squarely in a dramatic miscalculation.

Excessive Self-Disclosure

Foremost among the therapist's shortcomings that can lead to disaster are those that involve self-indulgence or excessive self-disclosure. Whether the therapist's ignorance, insensitivity, or narcissism is at fault, more than a few clients have been chased out of treatment because they felt negated by the repeated focus on the therapist's life. Under the guise of creating intimacy, closing psychological distance, modeling, or com municating empathic understanding, the therapist reveals so much about himself that the client becomes bored , feels ignored, or otherwise experiences feeling less important in the relationship.

Clearly the therapist's self-revelation can be a dramatic

i mpetus for breaking through a client's resistance, denial, and aloofness. It provides a means to create greater intimacy and bonding in the therapeutic relationship as well as exhibiting many qualities of sincerity and authenticity that are desirable to model in sessions. Yet even with all these powerful and useful attributes, self-disclosure remains one of the most abused interventions. Although confiding a brief anecdote about one 's life can be a most effective way to demonstrate a deep understand – ing of the client's concerns, a long-winded, tedious version wastes valuable time and negates the client's worth by sending a clear message about who is really important.

Therapists who talk too much about themselves frighten clients away by:

- Making them feel even less important as human beings. Already insecure and lacking esteem, clients feel even less worthy when the person they are paying for help communicates a disregard for what they have to say.
- Losing their own value as a neutral transference figure. There is a danger of becoming too human in a client's eyes—thereby losing one 's power to influence through modeling. If clients come to think, "Hey, this guy is just like me ," they may begin to wonder about the benefit of attending sessions.
- Boring the client to distraction. If there were ever an internati onal convention of ex-clients who got together to share t heir experiences, the most well-attended program would definitely be "My Therapist's Stories." More than a few clients have fled treatment because of terminal boredom with t heir therapist's repetitive anecdotes.

The truly sad thing about therapists who love to hear them – selves talk, whether it is in the client's best interest or not, is t hat they seem completely unaware it is a problem . And even if t hey are aware of their inconsiderate rambling, they enjoy it too much to stop.

One such psychiatrist was observed in the crowded lobby of a theater standing tall in his full-length mink coat, his pom – pous voice booming and ricocheting above the anonymous publie murmur. Suddenly his beeper emitted a high-pitched scream and those people who were not already watching his antics t urned to stare. With a flourish he consulted his gold Rolex, flicked back a misplaced lock of steel-gray hair, and strode in t he general direction of the telephone. The crowd parted as if t he Red Sea, and he quickly reached the phone area which was also quite congested. He advanced to the head of the line, im - patiently grunted aloud, and finally tapped the woman on the shoulder who was then using the phone. She glanced over her shoulder for a moment and then continued her conversation. By this time, the audience was quite amused by the show of watch - ing this pompous psychiatrist get snubbed. (His face was famil- iar to most because of his late-night television ads directing in- somniacs to visit his clinic.) Again he interrupted the woman with another tap on the shoulder. She covered the mouthpiece of the phone with her hand and disdainfully looked at this dis- ti nguished yet rude gentleman. "Madam ," he proclaimed in a voice as much for the audience as for her, "I am a doctor ." Without skipping a beat the woman sarcastically replied, "Your mother must be very proud ." As she went back to the phone, t he audience applauded enthusiastically, and the doctor slinked back to the end of the line.

While this is an extreme example of a level of arrogance we hope to avoid, many of us do lapse at times into a similar stance, if only for a moment. Sometimes we get carried away in our own self-absorption, talk to clients too much about our- selves, and inadvertently push them away in the process.

As Fisch remarked in the previous chapter, when he makes mistakes it is often because of his impatience. Not un - like the eager beginner mentioned in Chapter Five, we some- t i mes intervene too quickly before gathering all the necessary data and fully grasping the situation. We may miss some useful cues indicating the client's hesitance to follow a course of ac- t i on and therefore push too hard before the client feels ready. Our impatience may sometimes lead us to talk too much in ses- sions and end up in arguments with the client because we are working too hard to get the client to understand something.

Divulging too much of one 's life story, trying to convince

clients of what they need to do next, persuading them to see something the way the therapist does, all may begin in inno – cence under the guise of sincere helping. But overshadowed by t he therapist and pressured to conform , the client has little room for self-exploration, experimentation , or growth.

Misdiagnosis and Bungled Skills

It is not only the therapist's arrogance that can end treat – ment prematurely, but also the misapplication of techniques. Such a situation can stem from an initial misdiagnosis such as failing to identify some underlying psychopathology or organic dysfunction . But even with the most accurate assessment of a client's symptoms, the therapist may nevertheless bungle funda – mental helping skills. Here are some of the most common inter – ventions and mistakes that prematurely end treatment:

- Initiating confrontation in a manner that is perceived as too aggressive
- Venturing an interpretation that is too threatening for the client to deal with at the time
- Setting goals that are unrealistic or not consistent with the client's values
- Acting too passively in the sessions, failing to respond suffi – ciently to the client
- Failing to communicate adequate caring, respect, and accep – t ance in the therapeutic relationship
- Neglecting to establish a strong alliance with the client
- Crossing some boundary that feels invasive to the client's privacy or security
- Attempting paradoxical strategies, psychodramatic methods, or other powerful techniques that backfire
- Asking a series of close-ended questions in a style that may be experienced as inquisitorial
- Acting evasively or mysteriously in such a way that the cli – ent feels manipulated
- Responding with low-level empathic remarks that sound like parroting

- Mismanaging silence in sessions by allowing it to continue beyond reasonable limits

Of all the things a therapist can do to invite failure, Colson, Lewis, and Horwitz (1985) discovered that "inertial drag" plays the biggest part. Therapy often fails when the clinician is slow to recognize what clients require by underestimating psychopathology and then having trouble shifting directions. Other problems result when, in the name of patience and acceptance, t he therapist tolerates violations of the basic treatment contract. Lateness, skipped appointments, verbal assaults, noncompliance, delinquent payments, continued drug abuse—all show a neglect for the basic structure needed to make success possible. Some t herapists want so badly to avoid failure they will do almost anything to see a client on any terms—even if such a decision invites further inertial drag.

In the case Ellis presented in the previous chapter, a young man did not respond to therapeutic treatment because of an underlying endogenous depression that went undiagnosed for some time. For months Ellis attempted his most vigorous confrontations, but with little lasting effect. This type of misdiagnosis is particularly frightening because signs of underlying organic problems are often unclear even to psychiatrists, endocrinologists, and neurologists who spend their lives working in t hese areas. And those of us who are not medically trained simply do not know what to look for. What may appear to be a straightforward bout of anxiety, for example, with symptoms j ust like a hundred other cases we have seen, may in fact be signs of hyperthyroidism or any number of cardiovascular or neurological disorders.

The Therapist's Doubt

In his **Natural Science o f Stupidity**, Tabori (1959) catalogs instances from history in which otherwise learned men and women exhibited incredible rigidity and skepticism in the face of evidence that contradicted their beliefs. When a scientist or practitioner is confronted with data that do not fit his or her operating theories, there is a tendency to negate the results—an unfortunate decision that often leads to an impairment of long- t erm functioning, for such professionals do not significantly im - prove their effectiveness.

When the famous physician Jean Bouillaub was presented with Edison 's latest invention, the phonograph , he attempted to strangle the demonstrator, believing he was being deceived by ventriloquism . After he was eventually restrained, the good doc - t or addressed the assembly: " It is quite impossible that the no - ble organs of human speech could be replaced by ignoble, sense- less metal" (Tabori, 1959, p. 154).

The same sort of resistance, doubt, and denouncement re- sulted when Frangois Blanchard proposed launching the first hot air balloon in 1783 and, a month later, when a colleague at- t empted the first trip on a steam -engine boat: " But the pioneers of the railways fared no better   . o fficial science dismissed t hem with a sneer; said no railway engine would ever move, for t he wheels would keep on turning in the same place. . Ac- cording to the opinion of the Royal Bavarian College of Medi- cine, whoever traveled by train was bound to suffer concussion of the brain, while those who even looked at a train from the outside would faint with dizziness" (Tabori, 1959, p. 155).

Our own field has supplied enough of its own examples, for the skepticism and stupidity of its ruling majority have more t han once kept innovations in theory and technique from re- ceiving a fair appraisal. We should have learned by now that we can just as easily fail as "fools of doubt " as we can from impul- sive action. Failures in therapy sometimes occur not only by doing too much, but by doing too little. Those who are filled with doubt, who hesitate, who second-guess every decision and proceed cautiously trying never to make a mistake, end up short-changing both their clients and themselves for opportuni- ties to grow.

The therapist's doubt hampers his or her ability to take new roads, to experiment with new techniques, to be open to new contributions from colleagues. As described in Chapter Three, this resistance to change is best exemplified by those cases of failure in which the clinician, when faced with repeated disappointment in response to the same intervention, refuses to deviate from orthodox practice in the search for a creative solution.

Rigidity Versus Flexibility

The client-centered therapist nurtures a relationship for years, accepts unconditionally every facet of the client's behavior, reflects feelings, listens and responds empathically, but refuses to provide the structure that the client requires to become centered. The client feels loved in the sessions, but continues to flounder in life. The therapist yearns to confront the client's passivity and dependency , but feels that such a deviation would violate the basic tenets of therapy. The client genuinely likes the t herapist, so the option of going to a more directive practitioner is ruled out. Thus both condemn themselves to playing out eternally the same circular dance.

The cognitive-behavioral therapist disputes the client's irrational beliefs with eloquence and convincing evidence. She patiently identifies examples in the client's self-talk of self-inflicted misery. She presents elaborate refutations of the client's illogical thinking patterns. The client agrees they are brilliant insights, but somehow he does not feel any better. The sessions, although interesting and entertaining, only remind him of similar debates he once had with his mother. He only wants to be **understood.** If only he could just talk about his feelings, maybe
he could work things out for himself. He certainly understands the logic of the therapist's arguments, but rationality is not what he needs right now. The therapist senses the client's need t o explore this uncharted territory, but she cannot abandon the training that has, until now, served her so well.

The psychoanalytic therapist has made phenomenal progress in promoting insight within the client, who now clearly understands how she came to crave such abusive relationships in her life. She has meticulously dissected her history, learned about her defenses, studied her dreams, and attempted to strengthen her ego boundaries. Yet after five years of cooperati i on in her analysis, she still participates in many destructive encounters and has given no indication she is ready to abandon

them . Her therapist's passivity and withdrawal infuriate her —
not because they remind her of any single unresolved relationship from her past, but because she is tired of all the men in her
life treating her with indifference. If only the therapist could
make an effort to be a real person perhaps she could trust him
more fully. Until he gives a part of himself in a genuine way, she
has decided unconsciously to punish him by refusing to change.
The therapist, in turn , knows that an exploration of the dynam -
ics of their relationship would be fruitful, but he is too insecure
t o risk deviating from his detached posture.

These three examples illustrate the bind practitioners find
t hemselves in when they adhere strictly to a theoretical system
rather than allowing intuition and internal wisdom to assist in
dictating the   course of therapy. This dilemma was evidenced
in many of the beginners' tales of problems in therapy related in
Chapter Five. Moustakas also learned this truth early in his career, when in expertly employing the techniques acquired in
training, he practiced his craft with precision but lost the client
in the process. Failures occur not only when therapists depart
from the well-tested recipe for success, but also when they stub -
bornly conform to those instructions even under different con -
ditions with different ingredients.

Counter-Transference

In their study of treatment failures, Strupp, Fox , and
Lessler (1969) found that more than three-quarters of the cases
involved problems in the therapeutic relationship. Especially
prevalent are instances in which the clinician has failed to recognize his or her own issues as they pollute those of the client.

Bugental (1965) describes a case of failure in which he
neglected to recognize the extent of a client's existential crisis.
Although   therapist and client had worked well together, had
established a good therapeutic alliance, and had made headway
on characterological resistance and transference issues, things
nevertheless began to deteriorate at a critical point. In reviewing
his behavior, Bugental notes that he not only failed to grasp the
significance of a major life crisis, which he chose to interpret in a

superficial way, but his own counter-transference reactions re-stricted him from responding authentically: "Hindsight reveals i ntellectual competitiveness which resulted in the therapist being more reliant at times on documented argumentation than on personal confrontation —for this, and possibly other reasons, he tended to be more detached and more abstract than was re-quired " (Bugental, 1965, p. 17).

In combating failures that stem from the therapist's own counter-transference feelings, Robertiello and Schoenwolf (1987) urge the clinician to remain detached yet empathic in response to a provocative outburst: "To help a patient to be authentic again, the therapist must be authentic " (p. 10). But not in ways in which negative or unresolved feelings lead one to be aggressive, competitive, or vengeful against attacks that are misperceived as personally directed. Counter-transference can emerge from a sense of helplessness or waning control in the t herapist's life as well as other causes suggested by Masterson (1983) and Robertiello and Schoenwolf (1 9 8 7). We turn now to some specific examples.

Unresolved Feelings o f Abandonment. The therapist felt frus-t r ated throughout his childhood attempting to win his father 's attention and approval, but to no avail. He learned to be exces-sively conciliatory and reluctant to confront others —even when a client required a push to move forward. Because of a fear of rejection by his clients, especially those who were older men, t he therapist would hold back, play it safe, and refuse to con - sider evocative interventions. As a result, these clients would often "abandon " their therapy (and him) because of impatience and frustration with his lack of authentic responses.

Overdirectiveness. The therapist received little direction through - out her life from anyone —parents and teachers alike let her drift where she might, often floundering without structure or pur-pose. She stumbled upon the therapy profession just as she backed into relationships. All her life she had longed for some-one, anyone, to guide her in a particular direction. She attempted t o rectify the deficiency in her own life by overdirecting the

lives of her most passive, helpless clients. While some of these people did indeed respond well to her vigorous involvement, de - pendencies eventually ensued in many other cases. Therapy would sometimes fail as clients rebelled against the excessive control they felt by the concerned but overzealous therapist.

Overreaction. The therapist was undergoing a difficult divorce

and child custody fight in which her husband and his attorney were making life miserable by using threats, intimidation , and other legal tactics to disrupt her life and wear down her resis‐ tance. Enter a client, also an attorney , who exhibited many of t he characterological defenses helpful in that profession: The man was often evasive, manipulative, and vying for control of t he relationship. The therapy became combative as each party tried to score points against the opponent. The therapy ended after a particularly devastating salvo of insults (therapeutic con - frontations) was leveled at the distraught and defensive client.

Frustrated Love. The therapist was lonely and alone. His most

satisfying relationships were with his clients; in fact, that was t he only intimacy in his life. He was quite affectionate, even se‐ ductive, with his clients. He could be very flirtatious and end sessions with hugs. When his female clients professed their love for him and their desire to start a "real relationship ," he would i mmediately reject their advances—feeling quite satisfied with his restraint and professional integrity. Inevitably some of these women would fail to schedule another session.

Guilt. The therapist came from a strict Catholic upbringing and

a home in which his parents heaped guilt on him. Growing up he could rarely please his demanding mother and detached fa‐ ther. He could never seem to do enough. In rebellion against his overstructured Catholic education , he had adopted a client- centered therapeutic style that permitted him the freedom to respond permissively rather than in the critical ways he had ex - perienced as a child. One man he worked with was particularly hostile, resistive, and manipulative. He would attack the ther‐ apist, criticize his office, his clothes, his manner, his facial ex -

pressions, his interpretations and reflections. The therapist refused to be bated and simply tolerated the onslaught of abuse. He would not confront the acting out, but kept to his agenda of reflecting feeling—all the while feeling as guilty for his anger as he had as a child. The sadistic-masochistic ritual lasted until the client gave up in exasperation and fired the therapist, calling him a wimp.

The Need to Be Right.

The therapist attempted to deal with her underlying feelings of inadequacy by proving that she was the greatest therapist in the universe. She strove to make every intervention brilliant and poignant and kept a running score on how she was doing. One criterion of her superior skill and wit was the ability to win debates with her clients, to force them to see the truth of her arguments. She could be particularly devastating in her interactions with arrogant men:

Client: I'm not sure I agree with your assessment that my problem stems from

Therapist: Let me repeat what you 've been saying all along. You have clearly indicated

Client: Look, that 's beside the point. I'm sure that what I need to do right now is just the opposite of what you suggest.

Therapist: I must disagree. Your denial is clouding your judgment and I can prove it to you if you 'll just listen.

Client: Yes, well, go right ahead.

Patterns o f Error.

Each of these examples draws attention to some of the ways in which chronic factors sometimes result from the therapist's own resolved struggles and characterological defenses. There is a pattern for each of us in the typical errors we make, the situations we misjudge, and the cases we lose.

We do not work as hard for some clients as we do for others. Some people are even forced out of treatment when we grow tired of them . Feelings of anger or boredom or revulsion or fear or love provoke us to sabotage progress with certain clients. In subtle ways we withdraw , promoting feelings of reject i on in the client. Or we may needle our clients, pushing too hard because of our ambivalence regarding whether or not they return for more sessions.

Of course, the resistance, counter-transference, and block – age that we have identified in ourselves can be managed effec– ti vely through self-monitoring, supervision, and personal psy– chotherapy. It is the undiagnosed issues and disguised feelings t hat continue to create therapeutic failures. And it would be impossible to imagine that any therapist could be so thoroughly analyzed that even this very day or week or month some case was not bungled because of unrecognized and unresolved per– sonal issues.

When considering the multitude of forces that can im – pede therapeutic progress, it is a wonder that we experience relative success most of the time. As discussed in this chapter, many factors contributing to failure can be recognized and guarded against. It is equally important, however, to realize t here are probably just as many that are currently beyond our reach. Just as we need to know how to avoid failure when pos– sible, we also need to know how to live with it when it occurs.

Being a
Reflective Therapist

We have come to realize that failure is not only an inevi-t able component of therapeutic practice, but a potentially use-ful one in the learning and growth it can stimulate. Since it is the drive for perfection and the denial of fallibility that create the most problems for therapists and their clients, any strategy for dealing with negative results—both within sessions and with -in the clinician's mind —will have to take one 's attitude into con - sideration.

In a phenomenological description of his own emotional breakdown, a psychiatrist traces the roots of his problems to his self-critical and perfectionist nature. From such a personal fail-ure the doctor felt himself cleansed, enriched, and thereafter better able to understand and relate to his patients in a similar predicament: " It seems to me that from depression itself one learns nothing. Rather it is from what one makes of depression t hat benefit derives. Depression is depression. It lays waste and may prove, too, a total waste of time unless one uses the experi-ence, and all its consequences, to build anew " (Rippere and Wil-liams, 1985, p. 19).

Exactly the same interpretation of failure can be substi-t uted for this psychiatrist's view of his depression—it can be either debilitating or enriching. Throughout this book we have seen that failure need not be a diminishing experience. Indeed, we can regard it as an opportunity for expanding our repertoire of options. In the face of a client's resistance and defensiveness, some practitioners have used this impasse as a stimulus to de-velop ingenious therapeutic solutions. Hoffman, Kohener, and Shapira (1987), for example, describe a creative technique that emerged from work with therapeutic impasses. In an effort to reverse failure by getting at the client's overdependence, rejection, anger, and ambivalence, the authors experimented with two therapists treating a single, chronically resistive client. Rather than letting themselves feel discouraged by impasses, they discovered creative ways to counteract resistive behavior. They found that even with schizophrenics, passive dependent cases, and other difficult clients who had previously been inscrutable, dual therapist teams could be effective in a relatively short period of time.

When confronted with a hopeless case of retrograde amnesia from a degenerative brain disease, the pioneering neurologist A. R. Luria advised: "Do whatever your ingenuity and your heart suggest. There is little or no hope of any recovery of memory. But a man does not consist of memory alone. He has feeling, with sensibilities, moral being —matters of which neuropsychology cannot speak. And it is here, beyond the realm of an impersonal psychology, that you may find ways to touch him, and change him " (Sacks, 1985, p. 34).

The Reflective Therapist

Our field has seen an increase in the philosophy of pragmatism and the technology of eclecticism in the past several years. No longer satisfied with a single theoretical orientation , most clinicians now practice a form of helping that draws on the contributions from several different sources. Even the most orthodox psychoanalyst will use behavioral interventions when planning the sensate focus exercises of a sexually dysfunctional client. The strategic or behavioral therapist who focuses on symptoms will, nevertheless, work on building a client-centered relationship or exploring underlying psychodynamics. Four decades ago Fiedler (1950) observed that all effective therapists seem to do the same things in spite of their philosophical disputes. This convergence of universal principles is even more pronounced today and allows therapists to acknowledge failures and withstand them through a more flexible style of practice.

In the philosophy of pragmatism , as it was formulated by

Charles Peirce and William James at the turn of the century, the professional turns from contemplation , abstraction , imprecision, and rigid principles in favor of calculated action, flexible t hinking, effective intervention, and desired results. Pragmatism is concerned only with relative rather than absolute truth ; it is focused on useful knowledge that can be applied to specific situations. It is pluralistic, empirical, and practical.

Although it is not so concerned with philosophical assumptions or theoretical support, an eclectic orientation has been embraced by many practitioners who care less about the source of their inspiration than how to effect a cure. The eclectic therapist thus counteracts negative results by constantly ex perimenting with alternative strategies. The goal is "to use the common factors in psychotherapy as effectively as possible with all patients, while applying specific techniques to individual pa t i ents selectively, depending on the needs of the patient, the most appropriate techniques available, and the personality of the therapist" (Rubin , 1986, p. 385). Since the practitioner rarely feels trapped or runs out of options, failures can be minimized or overcome. With freedom to act in an endless variety of ways, the therapist need not feel helpless.

But technical eclecticism, while avoiding failure caused by ossified thinking or action, presents a number of problems for those who prefer a unifying framework. Flexibility may be quite useful to politicians who never wish to be accountable, but psychotherapy is not just an exercise in problem solving. Like most professions, it deals with issues that are unique, com plex, unstable, uncertain , and ambiguous. Whether in law, engineering, or psychotherapy , practitioners can indeed operate as technical experts, naming problems and then fixing them . But such an orientation to therapy fails to take into account the practical competence needed in situations where problems cannot always be fully named or solved.

Schon (1983) recommends an alternative to technical rationality that retains much of its pragmatic soul—and hence im munity to failure—but allows the professional to use an epistemology of practice implicit in a contemplative, creative, intuitive process. Since skillful practice involves knowing more than

we can ever say or do, the reflective practitioner relies on a certain reflecting-in-action: Actions and judgments are carried out
spontaneously, and the therapist is quite unaware how these
t hings were ever learned in the first place. This "tacit knowing"
was first described by Polanyi (1967) in considering how we
recognize a human face without being able to tell exactly how we
know it.

Schon goes on to develop his ideas of reflecting-in-action
by noting how jazz musicians or baseball pitchers or urban plan-
ners or therapists are able to improvise their performance, ad -
j ust to changing circumstances, and repeat those "pitches" that
have proved successful and avoid those that do not seem to be
working. When things are going the way we wish, we give no
t hought to the intuitive, spontaneous process that is occurring;
it is only when we encounter a surprise that we respond with
reflection-in-action: "A practitioner 's reflection can serve as a
corrective to overlearning. Through reflection, he can surface
and criticize the tacit understandings that have grown up around
t he repetitive experiences of specialized practice and can make
new sense of the situations of uncertainty or uniqueness which
he may allow himself to experience" (Schon , 1983, p. 61).

The pragmatic philosopher, the eclectic technician, the
reflective practitioner—all are able to deal with failure by adjusting their thinking and behavior. Less concerned with mulling
over endlessly, remorsefully, what exactly went wrong and ana-
lyzing the far-reaching implications of negative outcomes, such
practitioners help themselves cope with failure by focusing on
the practical considerations that will lead to future success and
more accurate predictions. Since this attitude is concerned with
positive results, no matter how this may be accomplished, feelings of inadequacy and insecurity that might undermine one 's
i ntuition must be ignored while the practitioner identifies the
obstacles that are getting in the way of success.

Since failure can occur only in a static situation in which
rules and definitions of success remain constant, Jenkins, Hildebrand, and Lask (1982) suggest a strategy for overcoming failure that involves constant reformulation of the problem based
on new information gleaned from the previous dead-end. The

first step requires the therapist to identify all those cues that in-
dicate failure is indeed occurring. What are the signs that therapy is not working? Whose perceptions appear to be valid regarding this determination ? What exactly does not seem to be
working?

The second step considers the reasons why therapy is not
proceeding in the desired direction:

- What secondary gains is the client celebrating as a result of
  t he failure?
- Has the problem been defined in such a way that it cannot
  be solved?
- What interventions have been most helpful? Least helpful?
- At which point did things begin slipping downward?
- Who has an interest in sabotaging the treatment?
- How have I been negligent?
- What may I have overlooked?

The final stage encourages the therapist to revise initial
t r eatment goals in such a way that they may be more easily
reached. If the therapist engages in constant reflection, unsuccessful therapeutic strategies can yield useful information leading to more effective predictions and interventions in the future.

In exploring the clinical relevance of pragmatism to psychoanalytic theory, Berger (1985) suggests that clinicians make
a shift from theorizing about pathology to a focus on therapy.
He believes the use of "thought experiments " would be a useful
t ool for examining specific empirical situations, encouraging
greater flexibility in thinking and acting on the part of the prac -
titio ner. "What I am suggesting as one possibility, then, is that
when a clinician poses a theoretical question, or asks for the
exact specifications of a concept, or proposes a research task,
t hese questions or proposals should be accompanied by a serious effort to demonstrate the clinical relevance of the request.
The clinician would have the task of projecting from proposal
t o possible outcomes, from questions to answer, and of demon -
strating how a given solution would affect practice " (Berger,
1985, p. 134). Pragmatism thus stresses the application of the -

ory to specific clinical situations. To conduct these thought ex‑ periments, the therapist would operate with maximum flexibil‑ i t y -letting go of ideas that do not fit or no longer work, creat‑ ing alternative constructs that might work better.

A Trusting Alliance

The opportunity to try multiple intervention strategies in a pragmatic, eclectic, or reflective style depends very much on t he client's indulgence and patience. Clearly, therefore, failures in therapy can best be prevented or at least processed with the client when there is a mutually caring and trusting relationship. As long as there is trust between client and therapist, there is t he time, the incentive, and the opportunity to work out any disagreement, rectify any error, and overcome any setback. As suggested by Langs (1978 , p. 185), it is essential to examine, with the client, the errors and misjudgments that sometimes t ake place during therapy. For here lie the seeds of growth and constructive change.

It is when the therapy is viewed only as a business pact or contractual arrangement (which it partly is), rather than an au‑ t hentic encounter between two people working toward the well‑ being of one of them , that the client is likely to seek redress or revenge if things do not work out. It is not just a matter of coin‑ cidence that certain professionals lose clients or get sued.

If intimacy has been firmly established in the therapeutic relationship, if the client feels respected, accepted, and valued, it is unlikely any single mistake can unravel all the progress. Still, even the most vigilant therapist may run into trouble. A psychiatrist who describes himself as careful, concerned, and cautious in his practice reflects on being sued unfairly by a patient: "My wife asked what on earth was the matter with me. She could see that I was down and that I had lost my appetite. In spite of my efforts to keep an even keel, I lost interest in so‑ cializing. Plans for dinner parties vaporized. My enthusiasm for fixing things and making improvements around the house van‑ ished. I could have cared less. I quietly ruminated , 'How could this have happened to me? How could this patient, whom I had done so much for, do this to me? What had I done to deserve this? Why me ? ' " (Powles, 1987, p. 6).

As a result of this single brush with a patient 's feelings of betrayal and subsequent revenge, Powles's practice became "tinged with a touch of paranoia ." He continues: "Thus far, t his experience has taught me how omnipotently I have practi ced, and how I have clung to the belief that 'good ' physicians can practice without making errors when they 're careful enough. But the events of the last few months have made it clear to me t hat I have engaged in, and supported , the myth of physician infallibility. I'm learning that making mistakes is not equivalent to i ncompetence but is an expected condition of functioning as a sentient being " (p. 7). Reflecting on his professional nightmare, Powles concludes that trust is the crucial value between doctor and patient: "Without trust, the contact becomes riddled with anxiety, thereby increasing the potential for anger, followed by blame and guilt. When trust does occur, we practice with less stress and are more inclined to spontaneously extend ourselves. In turn, our patients will reciprocate by working with us in a positive, cooperative manner " (p. 7).

Kouw (personal communication , 1988) tells us that it is essential to foster an alliance with the client so that goals for t herapy can be defined and assessed throughout the therapeuti c process. "The definition of goals for therapy then becomes a shared project and, in fact," he remarks, "often constitutes the t herapy for protracted periods." In this way therapists can acknowledge, from the start, both the benefits and the pitfalls of t herapy thereby affording them and their clients a realistic view of what to expect.

Reframing Failure as Success

One of the tribulations of an Outward Bound experience involves the completion of harrowing tasks that test one 's courage and resourcefulness. One obstacle requires you to enter a dark, dank cave alone, to feel along the slimy walls until you encounter a small, narrow passageway that can only be negotiated by squeezing through , and then making your way out to daylight.

A young woman stood just inside the cave gravely facing t he darkness within. Goosebumps dotted her arms, her breath ‑ ing became labored, and her heart pounded in her chest and her ears as she inched forward. Nightmares, long buried since child‑ hood , immobilized her so that she could barely move or even cry out for help. As a child she had been punished by being exiled to the darkness and dampness of her basement, alone t here to confront her terrors. And now all her fears returned.

After long minutes of forcing herself to proceed, fearful of what her peers and instructor would think if she failed to complete the obstacle, she eventually reached the hole. But she could go no further no matter how hard she tried. The darkness closed in around her, disorienting her, suffocating her to the point where she could hardly breathe. In terror, a scream escap‑ ing from her throat, she fled the cave in the direction she had come from . She ran, sobbing, into the arms and bewildered stares of her group who were waiting their turns.

A few hours later, after everyone else had finished the task, the leader began helping them process their experience. Several members discussed the things they had learned about themselves, the fears they had conquered . When the time came for the young woman to speak, she could not meet anyone 's eyes and still lay huddled on the ground. Before the silence had gone on too long, the instructor intervened: "I want to draw special attention to the courage you demonstrated in taking care of yourself the way you did. Rather than forcing yourself t o undergo an experience that was terrifying for you , and that obviously brought up a lot of pain from the past, you did just what you needed to do to survive. I, for one, would like to ap ‑ plaud your effort, and especially the way in which you recog‑ nized what you could handle and did not push yourself beyond t hose limits. We can all learn from your example ." As all the members clapped and cheered, the young woman lifted her head, a smile curling up the edges of her mouth . What, at first, appeared to be a heartbreaking failure ended up feeling like the culminating success of her life.

There are many instances that could be called to mind of apparent failures that turned out to be spectacular successes.

Many painful experiences—divorce, unemployment, rejection, embarrassment—promote growth and eventually come to be viewed as the impetus for other positive outcomes: a more loving marriage, a better job, greater self-awareness, more personal effectiveness. The key point, for our clients or ourselves, is that whether a situation is viewed as a failure or success depends very much on the interpretations we choose. Without resorting t o denial or rationalizing away results we dislike, it is still possible to look at a negative outcome as an "apparent failure," im - plying that the final evaluation is not yet in. Furthermore , there are many cases in which startling progress occurred months or even years after therapy terminated unsatisfactorily for the t herapist, the client, or both.

One couple had been in marriage counseling for over a year before they abruptly ended the sessions, angry at one an- other, and both of them incensed at their therapist. They filed for divorce and then sought individual consultations with the t herapist to express their rage and dissatisfaction with the way things were handled. The therapist, understandably, felt badly for them , but she wisely shrugged off her disappointment after reviewing her conduct. She had done all she could; the rest was up to them . She even had the presence of mind to suggest to the couple that what now seemed like a disaster to them might later be something they would feel very grateful for. Sure enough, months later, something clicked, some impasse was broken t hrough, and the couple returned to reconcile their differences. This is not such an unusual experience. It is just that we do not often follow up on our failed cases one, two, or five years later t o learn how things eventually worked out.

The Shrug

Gilbert Hill was the rising star of the Detroit Police De- partment. The top homicide detective and supersleuth of the area's unsolved kidnappings, murders, and rapes, he was pro - moted to inspector and then experienced a further meteoric rise in his career. Tapped to play Eddie Murphy 's boss in the popular film **Beverly Hills Cop** and its sequel, Hill became an instant celebrity. The mayor appointed him to head the Major Crimes Division, and it seemed there was no stopping the supercop from reaching stardom not only on the screen, but in his profession.

Then things fell apart. Gilbert Hill found himself in over his head as an administrator. During his brief tenure, the percentage of solved cases plummeted from 71 percent to 40 percent while his department's expenses skyrocketed. He was un-ceremoniously exiled from Police Headquarters to a desk job monitoring the department's horses, boats, and planes.

With remarkable candor, Inspector Hill remarked on his rise and fall: "Hell, I admit it," he says. "It was my own fault. I got blinded by the light. And I got dumb. Real dumb" (Beer, 1987, p. 110). Hill shrugs off his spectacular failure with an honest self-appraisal of his mistakes. "Truthfully, I was an average cop," says Hill. "I got a lot of publicity I did not deserve. . I'm happy where I am now," he insists. "It's the easiest job I ever had. I don't get called out at night. I don't have to look at dead bodies . . . I know how things look to others in the department. Hell, I admit it, okay? It was my fault. . But this ain't so bad. In fact, it's a damn fine job. I didn't do so bad after all. Hell, I'm still here, ain't I?" (p. 249).

Since mistakes are an inevitable part of any job, and success often depends on many random factors out of our control, shrugging off failures is a necessary skill. It is essential, that is, not to let oneself get bogged down with an error—rather, accept it, learn from it, and move onward without looking back. Among t he prominent therapists whose experiences with failure were described earlier, the ability to shrug off disappointment seems t o be a common denominator. Lazarus admits his frustration and pain yet forgives himself for being imperfect. Ellis, as well, accepts responsibility for his part in mishaps but vigorously t alks to himself in order to banish the idea of "total" failure from his vocabulary.

One of the things Ellis (personal communication, 1988) has pointed out is that by subscribing to irrational beliefs such as those we noted in Chapter One ("a failure with my client meant my personal failure as a therapist" [D.B.] or "with every client I must put myself on the line" [J.K.]), we create unnecessary anxiety regarding our performance. Ellis remarks that by unrealistically demanding to be absolutely perfect with every client all of the time we are setting ourselves up for a fall. In an article admonishing clinicians to be more forgiving of their fallibility, Ellis suggests that using self-talk to overcome irrational beliefs would be as valuable to us as it is to our clients: "When you ferret out the absolutistic philosophies and perfectionistic demands that seem to underlie your difficulties, ask yourself— yes, strongly ask yourself—these trenchant questions: (1) Why do I have to be an indubitably great and unconditionally loved therapist? (2) Where is it written that my clients must follow my teachings and absolutely should do what I advise? (3) Where is the evidence that therapy must be easy and that I have to en - j oy every minute of it? " (Ellis, 1985, p. 171).

Common examples of irrational beliefs that contribute to a therapist's stress and feelings of failure are supplied by Deutsch (1984, p. 839):

> I should be able to help every client.
> When a client does not progress, it is my fault.
> I should always work at my peak level of compe - tency.
> I am responsible for my client's behavior.

Besides the shrug and self-talk, our most famous colleagues employ other strategies that work for them in dealing with failure. Lazarus tries to work with modest expectations (going for a first down versus a touchdown). Ellis dispassionately and systematically studies his errors to learn from them , a practice also favored by Fisch. Since Fisch specifically defines success or failure as the resolution of a client's presenting prob - lem, his treatment outcomes become quite clear. He knows when he succeeds or fails; he has only to look at the glaring results. He thus spends a lot of time reviewing his cases with colleagues, soliciting comments, tracing the probable factors involved in negative outcomes. He does not allow himself to make excuses in order to escape responsibility. He does not like to fail but seems to mobilize his energy and motivation to work even

harder for his clients. To him it is essential to identify his mistakes so he does not repeat them in the future.

Gerald Corey distinguishes between making a mistake and
learning from it (an experience that is largely beneficial) and
failure (an experience that has a highly negative connotation). It
is the openness to growth after encountering a mistake that
makes failure avoidable for Corey. Although he cannot control
what clients do, or even the inevitability of occasional errors and
misjudgments, he can control the decision to examine his behavior in order to improve his effectiveness.

Processing Negative Feelings

One of the most universal supervision strategies focuses
the clinician's attention on her or his counter-transference reac-
t i ons that are blocking effective action. Corey and Corey (1988)
urge the therapist to get in touch with intense feelings toward the
client, biases, attitudes, fears, and present life conflicts that are
getting in the way. They then advise identifying the client's
projections and defense reactions that are interacting with our
own negative feelings.

Resistance can take many forms, of course, and clients
may sabotage their treatment for many reasons. They may be
reluctant to give up the secondary gains of their symptoms.
They may exhibit habitual helplessness and self-defeating behavior. They may externalize or intellectualize or passively with −
draw. They may attempt to overwhelm the therapist or avoid
change to the extent they will do almost anything to keep
things from progressing. At this juncture , the therapist often
views resistance as normal, necessary, even helpful, both to the
client in stalling for time and to the therapist in signaling that
t hey are exploring the right territory. When failure is treated as
a special case of managing resistance in general, then one pro −
ceeds just as one would with any impasse—getting a supervisor's
insights, increasing self-awareness of blind spots, working on un −
finished business that gets in the way.

Freudenberger and Robbins (1979), writing about the
general hazards of being a therapist, recommend that we take

several steps to metabolize the stresses and frustrations of our work. As in all instances of burnout, recovering from the specialized symptoms of failure is best handled by asking yourself certain questions: Are you free enough to let a client go when you are not interested in working with him? In other words, psychologically and financially, can you face the fact that some clients are just not right for you? In a passionate and articulate ending to their classic article, Freudenberger and Robbins conclude:

> However burned out we may become, we realize that we must prevent and overcome burnout and must regain our vitality and authenticity. We somehow know, within that part of ourselves that still retains our original impulse to serve humanity, that when we fail to serve the patients who come to us in need, we fail ourselves. That with this inner knowledge and awareness come the feelings of guilt and depression which further incapacitate us. Let us, then, pool our individual experiences wherever and however we can. Let us touch each other and share with one another whatever constructive thoughts we may have. Let us agree—intellectually — that honest giving does not deplete; that dishonest giving does deplete and promote depression, loneliness, and cynicism; and that we and our patients suffer equally when we fail ourselves. If we are to see the occupational life issues of our patients, perhaps a deeper look into our own house is the first order of business for all of us [197 9, p. 295].

Stone (1985), in his study of negative outcomes in psychotherapy, notes that while success may be seductive, failure is instructive (p. 145). In living productively with failure, it is this instructive quality that allows us to make the most of distressing and disappointing experiences and to herald the growth derived from a process of self-examination and discovery.

10

Learning from Failure
in Therapeutic Practice

It is quite customary to celebrate a victory. Winners are able to release excess energy, pat themselves on the back for a j ob well done, and reap the rewards of good cheer and fellowship. The defeated drag their aching bones back into the locker room and pout.

Given a choice between success and failure, who would not prefer the former? Losing is painful; it often represents wasted energy and time. Furthermore , failure provokes the ghosts of the past to come back and haunt us:

"I told you that you would never amount to much." " I knew something like this would happen."
" It 's your fault."
" If only you w eren 't so lazy."

Who ever heard of celebrating failure? What, after all, is there to commemorate? The answer to that question , presented through - out the book , is plenty.

In his book on the pursuit of ultra-solutions, Watzlawick (1988 , p. 101) explains the virtue of dead ends and failed efforts: "Mirages must be approached before they reveal them - selves as mirages. Wrong paths must be taken in order to dis- cover that they lead nowhere. This truism is in accordance with t he so-called constructivist view —the study of the processes by which we create our own realities. It postulates that all we can ever hope to know of the 'real' reality (if it exists at all) is what it is not. " He further points out that mirages fade as we ap- proach them and regain their sparkle only after we turn away from them . And so it is with any quest for understanding or resolution: Reality is ordered only after our constructions of it break down.

Failures are paradoxical in that they are often treated with revulsion even though they are necessary for discovering dead-end roads. If one has the appropriate mind-set:

Failure promotes reflection.

Failure stimulates change.

Failure provides useful information .

Failure gives feedback on the impact of action.

Failure encourages flexibility.

Failure teaches humility.

Failure increases resolve.

Failure improves one 's tolerance for frustration .

Failure fosters experimentation .

A Story of **Suicide**

One of the most horrifying failures that a therapist   (or any human being) could ever experience is losing a client through suicide. Not only is there nothing remotely redeeming about this act or its aftermath, but such failures are so devastating t hey can lead to total self-doubt, even end a career.

"Did I help ? " "Did it work ? " "What did he feel?" "Why did she say that ? " "What was really going on this morning ? " "What if . . . ? What i f . . . ? "   "Try this . . . ; no, try that . "   " If only ... If only   . . . " A nd, probably heaviest of all, "Was it really for the best? How do I know ? How can I be sure? God, it 's somebody 's life! " (Ram Dass and Gorman , 1985, p. 201).

To celebrate a failure is simply to respect what it can teach us. If there is any meaning to be wrested from the often senseless act of taking one 's own life, it is left to the living to find it.

Both of us authors have experienced this most painful of failures—a client's suicide. In fact, we came to write this book after a consultation in which one of us offered support to the other. Following is the story of how a client's tragic death pro ‐

voked a therapist's bewilderment, self-doubt, fear, despair, and, eventually, tremendous learning.

As I (D.B.) tell this story, I am very aware of how defen - sive I feel. I find myself wanting to rationalize the case, to ex - plain my behavior, to prove that I am competent and that I acted professionally. The client, Marcia, was a woman who en - t ered and reentered treatment with me several times over a five-year period. Each time she would come for a few sessions and t hen I might not see her again for six or eight months. The last t i me she began therapy, she was quite despondent and acutely suicidal. She showed all the usual warning signs indicating she was at risk and dealing with intolerable pain. I became so con - cerned that I referred her for a psychiatric consultation. The psychiatrist began treating her as well and prescribed antidepres- sant medication along with regular sessions.

Just prior to leaving on a three-week vacation, I saw Mar - cia for a session in which she disclosed her intense desire to die. I felt terrified for her and was especially concerned that I would not be there to help her. Yet I was aware she was seeing the psy- chiatrist on a regular basis, more frequently than she had been seeing me. That gave me some reassurance; it was going to be his problem .

I called the psychiatrist to communicate my concerns. I made appropriate arrangements, left on my trip with misgivings, but returned to phone her and find that she was quite fine. In our conversation she mentioned things were going well with the psychiatrist so she had no further interest in rescheduling with me.

On that very night Marcia went into her garage, took an overdose of medication that the psychiatrist had prescribed, and breathed in the lethal fumes of her idling car. I knew nothing about this for three weeks when the psychiatrist called to in- form me what had happened.

I went into total shock. I felt numb , paralyzed. I remem - ber exactly where I was sitting when he called. For several days I felt nothing at all. I insulated myself by concentrating on the dynamics of the case in an intellectual, detached way. That very day I drove to my office just to look at my records, to figure out what had happened. I had to know what I did or did not do, whom I had contacted , how I had described her symptoms. This task became of the utmost importance.

On some level, I felt responsible for her death. I had to convince myself it was not my fault, that the record would exonerate me. The next thing I did was confess—I called several colleagues to tell my story and found a lot of support and many similar experiences. I reminded myself I had acted appropriately and could conceive of nothing I could have done differently.

Then the grief began. I felt utterly sorry and sad. I felt utterly discouraged. I did not want to go into my office any more or see any other clients. I did not want to be in this profession. I did not want the responsibility for other people 's lives. 1 considered getting a real job with regular hours and few demands. I started to withdraw . I began doubting myself and every facet of my being.

Somehow , a few days later, I was back in my office seeing clients again. And in every single session I saw through the prism of my incompetence. My attitude became negative, my i nterventions tentative. 1 no longer felt useful. I languished and felt sorry for myself.

I did all sorts of reading about suicide. I talked with any one who would listen. I learned and relearned things I had known, but had let fall by the wayside. Then, shortly after that, an adolescent client began speaking of suicide. I panicked. I im mediately referred him elsewhere. I did not trust myself.

It has been some time since this incident, but even now I t end to overreact when a client mentions suicide. I freeze inside and struggle with the fear that once again a death may seem like my sole responsibility. But the resources I tapped when Marcia t ook her life now serve me well. Talking this out has helped im mensely. Getting supervision and insight from colleagues, hon estly sharing my feeling with others, has made all the difference. I no longer feel invincible . a nd that is probably the most significant truth I learned from this experience.

Not only have I benefited from struggling through this dark time, seeking help and support and confronting my own li mitations, but so have my students and colleagues. I first told

the story, hesitantly, to a class I was teaching on the psychotherapeutic process. It was a way, I suppose, of working it out, perhaps looking for compassion and understanding. At some level,
too, I believed it important for the students to bear witness to
t he event, to experience it with me, to know that this does indeed happen. While I feared, in the telling, I might expose my
i nadequacy as a therapist, the need to discuss it outweighed the
risk. As I had anticipated, the students rallied around me show -
ing compassion and concern. But, unexpectedly , they experienced a tremendous wave of relief. For in disclosing my fears
and frailties, I had tacitly given them permission to acknowledge their own.

With each telling of this story the same phenomenon occurs: not criticism or rejection but sighs of relief and expressions of appreciation and respect. Not only did I learn about my
own limitations and discover a multitude of resources to assist
me, I also learned that it is the sharing of our vulnerabilities that
t r uly allows us to make contact with one another.

The Therapist's Experience of Failure

The preceding episode vividly illustrates the benefits of
confronting failure. To encourage such self-reflection, we present here a summary of this book 's messages and a full descrip- t i
on of the therapist's experience of failure. We believe that fa-
miliarity with failure makes it more negotiable.

The first hint of something being amiss is an incongruence
between the therapist's expectations and the client's responses.
Therapists'   expectations are grounded in the nature of their
training, their experience, and the data collected through previous sessions. Also contributing to therapists ' mind-sets are the
t heoretical foundation , philosophical constructs, beliefs, and
values that comprise their orientation to the person and the
t r eatment. Operating concomitantly with this professional realm
of collected experiences are the therapist's life history and its
bearing on the present: Current concerns and struggles all con -
t r i bute to how therapists assess their work with clients. Of cen-
t r al relevance here, as well, is the therapist's level of self-esteem
and vulnerability.

In a moment of interaction with a person in therapy, a
t herapist receives what the client expresses through this filter
of personal and professional perceptions and experience and
activated awarenesses and needs. Through this complex prism is
filt ered the client's expression. When a therapist receives what
the client offers, a particular meaning is ascribed to the response
in terms of its fit with what the therapist believes should be occurring. This is the therapist's criterion, with or without the client 's participation, that has been set as an indicator of positive
outcome.

When the expression is discordant with a therapist's sense
of what should be occurring —and depending on the significance
of the particular expression to the therapeutic process as perceived by the therapist—feelings of confusion, frustration , and
disappointment are evoked. More attention is then brought to
t he moment in therapy in an effort to correct the disharmony.

Cognition becomes heightened as a therapist searches for
alternative understandings of the meaning of the client's expressions. At the same time, he or she begins to search for alternative ways of responding in order to bring the interaction in
line with the therapist's expectations. If this does not happen,
and there is continued departure from the therapist's goals, frus-
t r ation turns to anger directed either at oneself for being so limit ed in knowledge and vision or at the client for not responding
in a manner that lets the therapist know that he or she has succeeded.

The therapist struggles to make sense of the exchange, to
place it within his or her realm of knowledge and experience. If
t he therapist is unable to cast the experience within the con -
t i nuum of permissible or understandable behavior and responses,
if t he script becomes too deviant for the roles expected to com -
prise it, the therapist begins to feel the first flutters of self-
doubt. With heart thumping and mind racing, the clinician tries
harder to become reoriented in the moment in order to recap-
t ure a sense of equilibrium , direction , certainty.

At the moment of disequilibrium , of expectations being
unmet, some therapists, in their effort to make sense of what is
occurring, place the blame on the client and disown, completely,
t heir part in the unfolding drama. In so doing they can retrieve

t heir sense of balance and security and mask any feelings of responsibility. Other therapists, however, totally personalize what
is happening. They feel intense self-doubt and begin to engage
in harsh self-retribution. To deaden the pain of their misjudgments and faulty interventions, they often look outside of
themselves for solace. The tactics of self-deception all come into
play here: denial, rigidity, withdrawal, detachment, isolation,
and a myriad creative variations thereof —all geared toward re-
gaining a sense of balance within the self. The pendulum swings
between self-contempt and self-deception, between harshly con -
demning the self and angrily blaming the client, and each swing
paradoxically distorts reality and temporarily blocks a realistic
examination of the event.

Some therapists are stopped in their tracks by the thought
of failure. It is a guillotine cutting through the normal rhythm
and pace of their existence. A pressure is felt in their chests, a
leaden weight, a constant reminder that something is wrong. A
pervasive sense of self-doubt spills into every aspect of their
work. One 's ability as a clinician comes into question. Fantasies
of leaving the profession proliferate. Self-recriminations abound.
"I should have known ! " " I should have seen !" Anger and guilt
churn within as the therapist begins to acknowledge his or her
role in the troubling drama.

During the postmortem every act and statement is placed
under the microscope for careful study. All other clients seem
t o fade in the background , rendered almost insignificant by the
problem at hand. The therapist feels driven to sort through
every interaction with the client. Each is held up to the light,
examined, abandoned , then repeatedly brought forth for re-
examination. Books are read, colleagues consulted, all relevant
materials reviewed. The search continues until the therapist arrives at some grasp of what went wrong, owns and accepts his or
her part in it, and resolves to be different in the future.

The event no longer looms ghostlike in the therapist's
mind; the preoccupation with it recedes and now it takes its
rightful place alongside all the other therapeutic experiences ac-
cumulated to date. What remains is heightened awareness, a
dedication to continued learning, a willingness to be vulnerable,

and an appreciation for the mystery and adventure inherent in t herapeutic life.

Stages of Confronting Failure

From this description of the therapist's experience of failure we can discern five stages that seem to be inherent in the process of coming to terms with a disturbing therapeutic event. These stages are not the same as the developmental stages described in Chapter Two, which depict the central fears therapists confront as they progress from beginner to seasoned clinician. These, rather, are the stages therapists experience whether newcomer or veteran once failure has been realized. How readily practitioners move through these stages—or, in fact, how frequently failures are noted —may depend significantly on the person 's level of clinical experience and the definition used to determine a negative outcome . As emphasized in this book , t here is considerable variance among therapists in defining therapeutic failure.

The five stages are presented here to help therapists fully understand their experience of failure and thereby learn to cope with it: illusion, self-confrontation, the search, resolution, and application.

The period of **illusion** is a phase of denial in which therapists cast about for a source to blame other than themselves. This searching is perpetuated by the fear, anxiety, and guilt experienced with the awareness that something is not turning out as expected. It is in this stage that excuses and rationalizations prevail. The central theme is "it 's them , not m e ." Since the event is too painful to confront head-on, the ego seeks protec - t i on through a temporary distortion of reality.

Next anger with oneself creeps in and dispels the illusion t hat the other is at fault. This is the stage of **self-confrontation.** Now the therapist assumes total responsibility for what went wrong and painfully rakes the coals of self-recrimination and self-doubt. Every' aspect of the clinician's professional integrity is challenged.

This challenge activates the third phase—**the search,** a

need to find out what really went on. It yields to a more open and realistic seeking of information , a studying and scrutiny of t he event and its causes. Analogous to this searching phase is the data collection process in scientific research. In this case, how ‑ ever, the therapist, as researcher, seeks to uncover and explore every possibility through intense self-study and thorough access and tapping of all relevant resources. The findings from this re‑ search allow the therapist to discover significant dimensions of t he experience and put the event in a healthier perspective, thus attaining a sense of resolution.

In the next stage—resolution —the therapist, having opened
himself or herself to discovery, gains new insights about the event and identifies some new perspectives and direction. While t he therapist may never know exactly what went wrong, much has been learned in the searching process. The causes of the t r oubling event, whether resting with the therapist, the client, or both in combination , are placed in a manageable perspective. The therapist recognizes and accepts his or her part in the choreography of this particular therapeutic dance.

The final phase is an application of new learning in future
clinical work. The therapist feels a profound sense of commit‑ ment toward working more effectively along with an openness t o continued learning. The professional growth that emanates from confronting failure results in a sense of aliveness and pres‑ ence and an appreciation of one 's vulnerability. For it is only one 's vulnerability that paves the way for change and growth: "An experience of despair which tears a man out of himself and forces him to question the meaning of his existence can be a trigger for a new and authentic way of life" (Farnsworth , 1975, p. 46).

Questions to Ask Ourselves

In considering our vulnerability as therapists, there are questions we can readily ask ourselves to ensure we remain open t o an honest and forthright assessment of our work. It is through such self-scrutiny that we commit ourselves to continued learn‑ ing and growth. For each client consider the following:

- What are my expectations of the client? Of myself?
- What does the client expect of me? Of him- or herself?
- Are my expectations congruent with the client's expecta -
  ti ons?
- What is my investment in this case? What do   1 need from the
  client?
- How aware am I of the timing necessary for the process to
  unfold?
- What reaction is triggered in me by this client?
- What am I doing that is helpful?
- What am I doing that is not helpful?
- How may 1 be getting in the client's way?
- What changes can I make?
- What outside resources can I tap? Colleagues? Experts? Lit-
  erature?

By our willingness to examine our own work continually and honestly admit our own vulnerabilities, we activate a pro - cess that makes us receptive to new information and eager for discovery. This is especially true in the personal definitions we use for success and failure.

Failure is a judgment—a personal interpretation of an out - come based upon expectations. It is, therefore, the prerogative of every therapist to define his or her process (rather than eval- uating isolated performance) according to individual values, goals, and beliefs. In examining the theological aspects of cop - ing with failure, for example, Malcomson (1977) lists several criteria by which he judges success or failure. Although Mal- comson is quite hard on himself—he is inclined to measure his successes and failures in terms of single accomplishments (" I am a failure when I feel that I am overwhelmed ")—he does in- t r oduce one process-oriented criterion that is helpful in being more self-forgiving: He feels successful when he is doing some- t hing that feels important; he has failed if what he is doing does not seem to amount to anything.

The key words in this statement are "feels" and "seem ." For it is within our power, regardless of how an intervention, a session, or a therapeutic relationship turns out, to determine

how we wish to feel about it and whether we wish to give ourselves credit for our loving intentions and authentic desire to be
of assistance. It is difficult to fail as long as we continue trying
t o be helpful. In Malcomson 's words: "The failure is not so
much a failure to accomplish a task as it is a failure to care
deeply about a person " (p. 179). As long as we act in reasonably responsible ways, do the best we can with what we know at
the time, and deeply care about our client, failure or success
becomes less important than the continuing process of living,
growing, being.

   This is not to say that doing good therapy is simply a
matter of caring. Rather, effective clinicians are not only highly
skilled and wise but also accepting of the imperfections in oth - ers
as well as those in themselves. They examine their limita- tions,
acknowledge their errors and misjudgments, and, most of all, work
hard to avoid repeating them .

   Afterword : The Experience of Writing This Book

   Creating this work has been an extremely painful process for
us. At first we were filled with joy —at the prospect of pub - li
shing our thoughts on very personal issues and sharing a proj- ect
that could only strengthen our friendship.

   But things soon turned sour. We avoided one another, we
worked in isolation. When we absolutely had to meet, it felt like
a chore rather than the joyous lunches we had celebrated previously. The pages kept being written , chapters completed on
schedule, but never with much satisfaction. Not only was the
subject painful and depressing, but it started to pollute our rela-
t i onship.

   Performance anxieties emerged and, at one point, an aw -
ful fear of failure. The writing was flowing for Jeffrey, but
Diane felt blocked. Attempting to help one another only seemed
t o intensify our mutual frustration . The project felt doomed ,
our spirits depleted. In exasperation Diane, consumed with her
sense of failure in not being able to satisfy her own expecta -

tions, resigned from the commitment. She felt relieved, free, t r ue to her integrity in not having her name on the cover of a book to which she had not contributed to her satisfaction. Jeffrey, too, felt released from the tension between them . Perhaps their friendship could now resume. Yet there was sorrow and guilt and resentment and frustration and, yes, feelings of failure. There was incredible resistance to completing the project. Jeffrey wanted just to be done with it. Diane preferred to drop it and get on with something else ——anything else. Yet she

persevered and overcame her resistance. With the blocks gone, words and paragraphs finally flowed.

Thus we have struggled with this topic and with ourselves. Each of us has failed a dozen times—when the words would not come, when doubt silenced our inner voice, when the t ension between us threatened our mutual comfort. To be hon est, if we had known what was at stake, what risks were in volved in getting so close to this subject, we might never have been so rash as to attempt it.

Yet it is done. And we celebrate this completion with t r emendous ambivalence. It feels less like having a baby than it does like having a tumor excised. Now we understand why t herapists hate talking about this taboo subject and why the literature ignores it. It is painful, very painful, to relive those ex periences we would most like to forget. And yet we feel free now. Things are out in the open for all to see. We are all imperfect. We make mistakes. We learn from these errors . . . and still continue to find new ways to fail.

Our sincere hope is that you , the reader, can do what we, for so long, could not ——forgive yourself for being human , open yourself up to studying your mistakes and misjudgments, and celebrate your failures as opportunities for increased personal and professional mastery.

References

Alonso, A. The Quiet Profession: Supervisors o f Psychotherapy. New York: Macmillan, 1985.

Anderson, C. "The Crisis of Priorities." Family Therapy Networker, May -June 1987, pp. 19-25.

Armour, R. "Introduction ." In P. Tabori, The Natural Science o f Stupidity . Philadelphia: Chilton, 1959.

Barbrack, C. R. "Negative Outcome in Behavior Therapy ." In D. T. Mays and C. M. Franks (eds.), Negative Outcome in Psychotherapy and What to Do A bout It. New York: Springer, 1985.

Beer, M. "Exile on Beaubien Street." Detroit Monthly, September 1987, pp. 108 -1 1 0 .

Bergantino, L. "Human Relationships Are Destined to Failure ." Psychotherapy: Theory, Research and Practice, 1985, 72 (1), 42 - 4 3 .

Berger, L. S. Psychoanalytic Theory and Clinical Relevance. Hillsdale, N.J.: Analytic Press, 1985.

Boorstein, D. The Discoverers. New York: Random House, 1983.

Bugental, J.F.T. Challenges o f Humanistic Psychology. New York: McGraw-Hill, 1957.

Bugental, J.F.T. "The Existential Crisis in Intensive Psychotherapy ." Psychotherapy, 1965 ,2(1),16-20.

Bugental, J.F.T. The Search for Existential Identity . San Francisco: Jossey-Bass, 1976.

Bugental, J.F.T. Psychotherapy and Process. Reading, Mass.: Addison-Wesley, 1978.

Bugental, J.F.T. The Art o f the Psychotherapist. New York: Norton , 1987.

Clark, R. W. Einstein. The Life and Times. New York: Avon, 1971.

Coleman, S. (ed.). Failures in Family Therapy. New York: Guil-

ford, 1985.

Colson, D., Lewis, L., and Horwitz, L. "Negative Outcome in Psychotherapy and Psychoanalysis." In D. T. Mays and C. M. Franks (eds.), Negative Outcome in Psychotherapy and What to Do About It. New York: Springer, 1985.

Conroy, P. The Prince o f Tides. Boston: Houghton Mifflin, 1986.

Corey, G. Theory and Practice o f Counseling and Psychother- apy. (4 th ed.) Monterey, Calif.: Brooks/Cole, in press.

Corey, G., and Corey, M. S. Helping the Helper. Monterey, Calif.: Brooks/Cole, 1988.

Corey, G., and Corey, M. S. / Never Knew I Had a Choice. (4 th

ed.) Monterey, Calif.: Brooks/Cole, in press.

Denton, L. "Committee Developing Handbook on Helping Im - paired Colleagues." APA M onitor, 1987, 18 (10), 2 0 -2 1 .

Deutsch, C. J. "Self-Reported Sources of Stress Among Psycho- t herapists." Professional Psychology, 1984, 15 (6), 8 3 3 -8 4 5 .

Eckert, A. The Court Martial o f Daniel Boone. New York: Ban-

tam, 1973.

Einstein, A., and Infeld, L. The Evolution o f Physics. New

York: Simon & Schuster, 1938.

Ellis, A. "How to Deal with Your Most Difficult Client—You ." Psychotherapy in Private Practice, 1984, 2 (1), 25 -3 4 .

Ellis, A. Overcoming Resistance. New York: Springer, 1985.

Farber, B. A. (ed.). Stress and Burnout in the Human Service Professions. New York: Pergamon, 1983.

Farnsworth , K. E. "Despair That Restores." Psychotherapy. Theory, Research, and Practice, 1975, 12 (1), 4 4 - 4 7 .

Fiedler, F. "A Comparison of Therapeutic Relationships in Psy-

choanalytic, Non-Directive and Adlerian Therapy ." Journal o f Consulting and Clinical Psychology, 1950, 14, 436.

Fine, H. J. "Despair and Depletion in the Therapist." Psycho -
therapy: Theory, Research and Practice, 1980, 7 7
(4), 392—
395.
Fisch, R., Weakland, J. H., and Segal, L. The Tactics o f
Change: Doing Therapy Briefly. San Francisco:
Jossey-Bass, 1982.

Foa, E. B., and Emmelkamp , P.M.G. Failures in Behavior Ther- apy. New York: Wiley, 1983.

Frazer, A., and Winokur, A. "Therapeutic and Pharmacological Aspects of Psychotropic Drugs." Biological Basis o f Psychi- atric Disorders. Jamaica, N.Y.: Spectrum , 1977.

Freudenberger, H. J., and Robbins, A. "The Hazards of Being a Psychoanalyst." Psychoanalytic Review , 1979, 66 (2), 275 - 296.

Glasersfeld, E. von. "An Introduction to Radical Construc- t i vism ." In P. Watzlawick, The Invented Reality. New York:
Norton , 1984.

Goertzel, M., Goertzel, V., and Goertzel, T. Three Hundred Emi- nent Personalities: A Psychosocial Analysis o f the Famous.
San Francisco: Jossey-Bass, 1978.

Goleman, D. Vital Lies, Simple Truths. New York: Simon & Schuster, 1985.

Graziano, A., and Bythell, D. L. "Failures in Child Behavior Therapy ." In E. Foa and P. Emmelkamp (eds.), Failures in Behavior Therapy. New York: Wiley, 1983.

Greenspan, M., and Kulish, N. M. "Factors in Premature Termi- nation in Long-Term Psychotherapy ." Psychotherapy: The- ory, Research and Practice, 1985, 22 (1), 7 5 -8 2
.

Guy, J. D. The Personal Life o f the Psychotherapist. New York: Wiley, 1987.

Haley, J. "How to Be a Marriage Therapist Without Knowing Practically Anything ." Journal o f Marital and Family Ther- apy, 1980, 6, 385 -3 9 1 .

Hammer, M. (ed.). The Theory and Practice o f Psychotherapy with Specific Disorders. Springfield, 111.: Thomas, 1972.

Hayward, J. W. Perceiving Ordinary Magic. Boston, Mass.: Shambhala Publications, 1984.

Heilman, I. D., Morrison, T. L., and Abramowitz, S. I. "Ther - apist Flexibility/Rigidity and Work Stress." Professional Psy- chology, 1987, 18 (1), 21 -2 7.

Herron, W. G., and Rouslin, S. Issues in Psychotherapy. Wash- i ngton, D.C.: Oryn Publications, 1984.

Hilfiker, D. "Making Medical Mistakes." Harpers, May 1984, pp.
180

59 -6 5.

Hilfiker, D. Healing the Wounds. New York: Pantheon , 1985.

Hobman, D. L. "Failure." Hihhert Journal,   1953 -5 4 , 52,
    178—

185.

Hobson, R. F. Forms o f Feeling: The Heart o f
Psychotherapy.

New York: Tavistock, 1985.

Hoff, B. The I'ao o f Pooh. New York: Penguin, 1982.

Hoffman, S., Kohener, R., and Shapira, M.   "Two on One: Dia-
    lectical Psychotherapy ." Psychotherapy,   1987,   24 (2),212 -
216.

Hyatt, C., and Gottlieb , L. When Smart People Fail. New
York:

Simon & Schuster, 1987.

Jackel, M. "Supervision in Dynamic Psychotherapy ." In M. Blu-
    menfield (ed.), Applied Supervision in
Psychotherapy. New

York: Grune & Stratton , 1982.

Jenkins, J., Hildebrand, J., and Lask, B.   " Failure: An Explora-
    t i on and Survival Kit ."Journal o f Family Therapy, 1982,
                                                4,

307 -3 2 0 .

Jung, C. G. Memories, Dreams and Reflections. New
York: Ran -

dom House, 1961.

Keith, D. V., and Whitaker, C. A.   "Failure: Our Bold Com -
    panion ." In S. Coleman   (ed.), Failures in Family
Therapy.

New York: Guilford, 1985.

Keyes, R. Chancing It: Why We Take Risks.
Boston: Little, Brown, 1985.

Kilburg, R. R. "The Distressed Professional: The Nature of the
Problem ." In R. R. Kilburg, P. E. Nathan , and R. W. Thore-
son (eds.), Professionals in Distress: Issues,
Syndromes, and Solutions in Psychology.
Washington, D.C.: American Psy- chological Association, 1986.

Kilburg, R. R., Nathan, P. E., and Thoreson, R. W.   (eds.). Pro-
    fessionals in Distress: Issues, Syndromes,
    and Solutions in Psychology. Washington, D.C.:
American Psychological Asso- ciation, 1986.

Kottler, J. A. Pragmatic Group Leadership. Monterey,

Brooks/Cole, 1983.

Kottler, J. A. On Being a Therapist. San Francisco: Jossey-Bass, 1986.

Kramer, R. "Values of Error." Psychiatric Times, January 1987.

Langs, R. Techniques in Transition. New York: Jason Aronson, 1978.

Levinson, P., McMurray, L., Podell, P., and Weiner, H. "Causes for the Premature Interruption of Psychotherapy by Private Practice Patients." American Journal o f Psychiatry, 1978, 135 (7), 8 2 6 -8 3 0 .

Lowen, A. Narcissism. New York: Macmillan, 1983.

McMurtry, L. Lonesome Dove. New York: Pocket Books, 1986.

Madanes, C. Strategic Family Therapy. San Francisco: Jossey-Bass, 1981.

Malcomson, W. "Being vs. Doing: A Way of Coping with Success and Failure." Humanitas, 1977, 13 (2),169-18 3 .

Margolis, J. "Actions and Ways of Failing." Inquiry, 1960, 3, 89 -1 0 1 .

Martin, E. S., and Schurtman , R. "Termination Anxiety as It Affects the Therapist." Psychotherapy: Theory, Research and Practice,1985, 22 (1), 9 2 -9 6 .

Martz, L. "America Grounded ." Newsweek, August 17, 1987, p. 34.

Maslach, C. Burnout. The Cost o f Caring. Englewood Cliffs, N.J.: Prentice-Hall, 1982.

Masterson, J. F. Countertransference and Psychotherapeutic Technique. New York: Brunner/Mazel, 1983.

Mays, D. T., and Franks, C. M. "Negative Outcome: Historical Context and Dysfunctional Issues." In D. T. Mays and C. M. Franks (eds.), Negative Outcome in Psychotherapy and What to Do A bout It. New York: Springer, 1985.

Menaham , S. E. "Psychotherapy of the Dead ." In G. C. Ellenbogen (ed.), Oral Sadism and the Vegetarian Personality. New York: Ballantine, 1986.

Millon, T., Millon, C., and Antoni, M. "Sources of Emotional and Mental Disorders Among Psychologists: A Career Development Perspective." In R. R. Kilburg, P. E. Nathan, and R. W. Thoreson (eds.), Professionals in Distress: Issues, Syn - dromes and Solutions. Washington, D.C.: American Psycho- logical Association, 1986.

Murchie, G. The Seven Mysteries o f Life. Boston: Houghton Mifflin, 1978.

Polanyi, M. The Tacit Dimension. New York: Doubleday, 1967.
Powles, D. E. "Me Get Sued . . . Are You Kidding ?" Psychiatric
    Times, January   1987, pp. 1-7.

Ram Dass and Gorman , P. How Can I Help? Stories and Reflec - tions on Service. New York: Knopf, 1985.

Rippere, V., and Williams, R. Wounded Healers: Mental Health Workers' Experience o f Depression. New York: Wiley, 1985.

Robertiello, R. C., and Schoenwolf, G. 101 Common Therapeu - tic Blunders. Northvale, N.J.: Jason Aronson , 1987.

Rochlin, G. Griefs and Discontents. Boston: Little, Brown, 1965.

Rubin, S. S. "Ego-Focused Psychotherapy: A Psychodynamic Framework for Technical Eclecticism ." Psychotherapy, 1986, 23 (3), 3 8 5 -3 8 9 .

Sacks, O. The Man Who M istook His Wife fo r a Hat. New York: Harper, 1985.

Schlight, W. J. "The Anxieties of the Psychotherapist." Mental Hygiene,   1968, 52, 439 - 4 4 4 .

Schon, D. A. The Reflective Practitioner. New York: Basic Books, 1983.

Scott, C. Boundaries in Mind. New York: Crossroads,1982.

Shem, S. line . New York: Dell,1985.

Stoltenberg, C. D., and Delworth, U. Supervising Counselors and Therapists A Developmental Approach . San Francisco: Jossey-Bass, 1987.

Stone, M. "Negative Outcome in Borderline States." In D. T. Mays and C. M. Franks (eds.), Negative Outcome in Psycho - therapy and What to Do A bout It. New York: Springer, 1985.

Strean, H. S., and Freeman, L. Behind the Couch. Revelations o f a Psychoanalyst. New York: Wiley, 1988.

Strupp, H. H. "On Failing One 's Patient." Psychotherapy. The - ory, Research and Practice,   1975, 12 (1), 39 -4 1 .

Strupp, H. H., Fox, R. E., and Lessler, K. Patients View Their Psychotherapy. Baltimore: Johns Hopkins, 1969.

Strupp, H. H., and Hadley, S. W.   "Negative Effects and Their

Determinants." In D. T. Mays and C. M. Franks (eds.), Negative Outcome in Psychotherapy and What to Do About It. New York: Springer, 1985.

Stuart, R. B. Trick or Treatment. Champaign, Ill.: Research Press, 1970.

Tabori, P. The Natural Science o f Stupidity . Philadelphia: Chilton, 1959.

Theobald, D. W. "Errors and Mistakes." Dialogue, 1979, 18, 555-565.

Thomas, L. The Medusa and the Snail. New York: Viking, 1979.

Torrey, E. F. Witchdoctors and Psychiatrists. New York: Harper & Row, 1986.

Van Hoose, W. H., and Kottler, J. A. Ethical and Legal Issues in Counseling and Psychotherapy: A Comprehensive Guide. (2 nd ed.) San Francisco: Jossey-Bass, 1985.

Watzlawick, P. Ultrasolutions. New York: Norton , 1988.

Watzlawick, P., Weakland, J. H., and Fisch, R. Change: Princi- ples o f Problem Formation and Problem Resolution. New York: Norton , 1974.

Wedding, D., and Corsini, R. J. (eds.). Great Cases in Psycho - therapy. Itasca, 111.: Peacock, 1979.

Wenegrat, B. Sociobiology and M ental Disorders. Menlo Park, Calif.: Addison-Wesley, 1984.

Zukav, Ci. The Dancing Wu L.i Masters. New York: Bantam , 1979.

Index

189